The Employee Motivation Audit

An eight-step audit to determine how well equipped you are to win and retain employee commitment

Jane Weightman

CSP

Cambridge Strategy Publications Ltd.
Station Offices
Station Yard
Axminster
Devon. EX13 5PF
United Kingdom

www.cambridgestrategy.com

CONTENTS

Second Edition: 2008

ISBN 978-0-9559707-0-2

What Will You Get From This Audit?

We all know the pleasure of working with enthusiastic colleagues to get something worthwhile done. The buzz of excitement, the sense of innovation, the delight in our achievement; and we are paid as well! We are truly motivated at work and committed to getting things done.

When people are not committed to what they are doing their work can begin to grow poor. The quality and quantity suffer, people become less flexible and their time-keeping gets slack, they are off sick more frequently and they start looking for other employment. Where a whole group of workers feel like this an organisation can soon lose confidence and everyone wonders what went wrong. Some will blame the economic environment, some the management, and some will say the workers were poorly motivated.

What is employee motivation? In this guide I hope to show you that it is all the factors that go towards ensuring that individuals contribute their best work because they feel it is in their interest to do so, to the standards set for the rewards offered. Employee motivation includes understanding individual differences and organisational factors that interact with each other to produce a committed, highly motivated workforce who achieve an excellent performance.

This audit is really an overview or diagnostic device to help you see how different aspects of the organisation might affect the commitment of your employees.

Objectives

1. To understand what motivates employees at work.
2. To be able to analyse your own organisation's approach to employee motivation.
3. To understand how the interaction between various aspects of the organisation can support or hinder employee motivation.

4. To appreciate that different organisations need to attract different sorts of employees and that each organisation needs to attract different employees to give committed performances. This means there is no simple "motivator" of people at work.

Benefits from this Approach

1. Understand some of the main models and views about employee motivation.
2. See how to apply them to your organisation.
3. Motivate employees better and encourage them to give a more committed performance.
4. Use the summary statements and audit questions to conduct a quick review of your organisation's current approach.

The Audit's Structure

This audit is structured in three parts. Part 1 looks at the different theoretical approaches to employee motivation. Part 2 presents the audit itself with a series of questions for each of the eight steps. Part 3 looks at the audit process and presents a framework within which to conduct a well-structured audit.

Part 1

What are the Ways of Motivating Employees?

PEOPLE WANT DIFFERENT THINGS

In common parlance we often say things like "Jim is motivated by money" or "Jane really enjoys competition." The assumption is that we can see motivation. The reality is that we can only hypothesise that someone is motivated by some particular thing by looking at their behaviour and seeing if there is anything different when the particular "thing" is involved. Motivation is not something we can feel, smell, hear or see; we can only see the consequences of someone's inner motivation. Motivation is a drive within a person to try to achieve a goal, to meet a want or need.

We use the words "motivation", "wants", "needs" and "motives" freely both at work and elsewhere. We talk of Pat having the motivation to get on. We talk to Winston about wanting promotion. We listen when Chee says he needs the project. We discuss with Ikbahl other people's motives for doing things. All these attributes have to be deduced from their behaviour. We are in reality guessing at what motivates people from the way they behave in different circumstances.

Motivating people at work is not just a case of pressing the right button to switch them on, no matter that some managers feel this is how it should be. Indeed managers cannot technically motivate people, as it is an internal state that directs people towards certain goals or objectives. The management task is to ensure that each individual's motivation is engaged by checking that they are willing to work, to a standard, for the rewards offered. It is important to understand this distinction as many managers treat everyone the same and try to manipulate people by trying to "motivate" them. A better way is to try to understand the needs and objectives of those who work for or with you and arrive at some sort of equitable arrangement that their needs as well as the organisation's needs will be met.

This is sometimes enshrined in the phrase "the employment (or psychological) contract". This contract involves a series of expectations between the individual member and the organisation. These expectations are not defined formally and the individual and the organisation may not be conscious of the contract, but the relationship is affected by the expectations. This means taking into account individual differences in how they interpret the rewards offered. For example, we will all differ in our interests, attitudes and needs. That will affect how we react to different aspects of the job, such as its degree of autonomy, variety and amount of work to be done. We will also react differently to the work environment of peers and supervision and the organisational climate. We all have different reasons for going to work and we want different things from work. Some of us are looking for totally involving jobs that offer opportunities for responsibility and recognition, for example becoming general managers. Others are looking for a little more money and the freedom to get on with things away from work. That is, we have different attitudes to work.

As well as the differences between individuals, there are also broader, generational differences. Much recent research (for example the Talentsmoothie report *Generation Y: What they want from work*) has highlighted this. 'Gen Y' employees (born since 1980) tend to value excitement, engagement, flexibility and opportunities for personal development at work more highly than older generations do.

Understanding the motivation of people at work means admitting that different things will have different values to different people. This suggests that we need to understand that those who work with us may not have the same orientation to work as ourselves. To paraphrase C.W. Mills (author of *White Collar*):

> *Work may be a mere source of livelihood, or the most significant part of one's inner life; it may be experienced as hard graft, or as an exuberant expression of self; as a bounden duty, or as a development of man's universal nature. Neither love nor hatred of work is inherent in man, or inherent in any given line of work.*

An example of the different approaches to work can be seen when some people opt for part-time, temporary or contract work, so-called periphery work. Others opt for permanent, full-time work, so-called core work. This can be an expression of a different set of priorities as well as the available opportunities.

Maslow's Model of Motivation

Psychologists have studied the behaviour of animals and humans to try to find out what things people will work for — what gives pleasure and what inhibits behaviour. The most famous model of the variation in motivation across time, for the same person and between people is that of Abraham Maslow, see Figure 1. He grouped needs into a hierarchy of five stages. The first two he called primary needs, concerned with our basic physical requirements. The latter three stages he called secondary needs: these are learned, psychological needs which only come into play when the primary needs are satisfied, and are more culturally determined. For example, if we are hungry or physically exhausted we are less concerned about being free from pain or secure. He also pointed out that once a primary need is satisfied it loses its potency and is no longer a motivator. So in our example, once the hunger or exhaustion is satisfied the person will be less motivated by food and rest and will be more motivated to seek safety. By contrast, Maslow argues, secondary needs continue to motivate and we seek more of them even when we have experienced some satisfaction of this need.

At work, at least in the developed world, most of us have our primary needs satisfied by regular periods of rest and food, with sufficient shelter to protect us from the climate. Just think of the fuss we make when the heating or air-conditioning is

FIGURE 1
MASLOW'S HIERARCHY OF HUMAN NEEDS

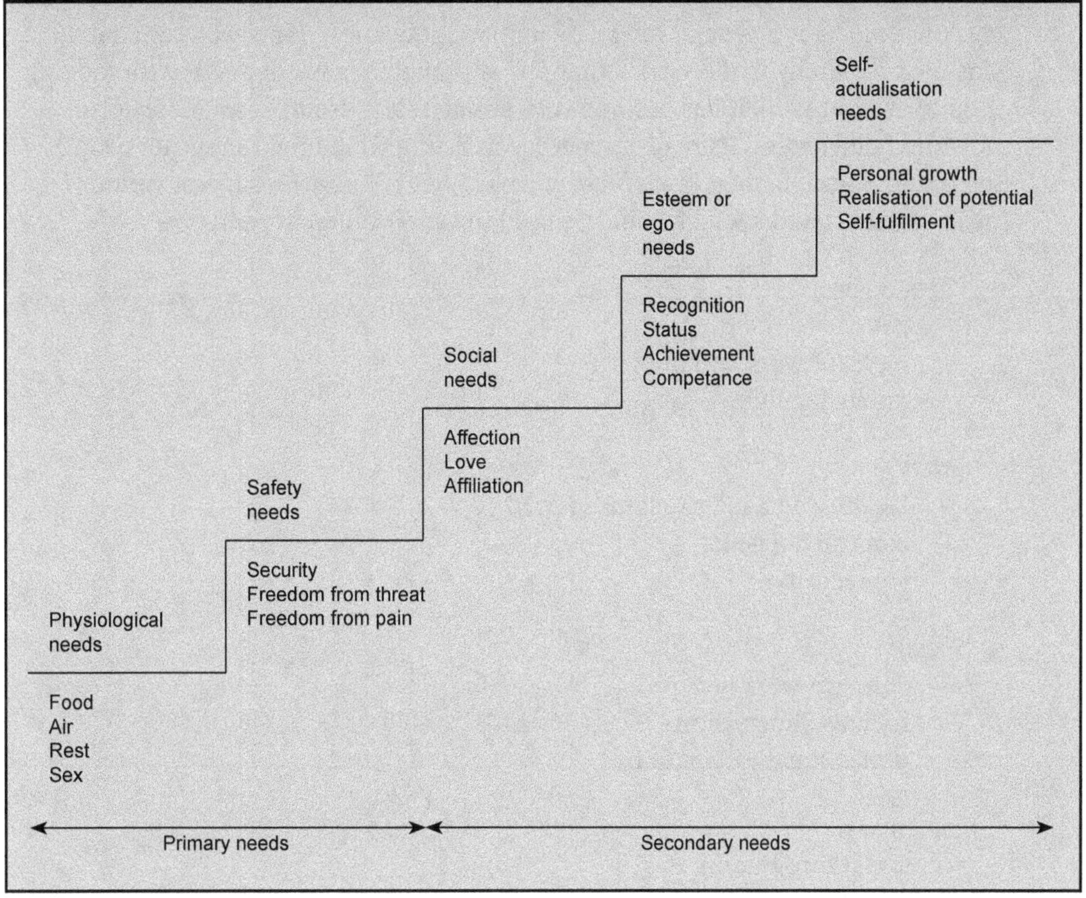

not working. In analysing the behaviour in western organisations we are mostly concerned with the motivation based on secondary needs. Many organisations recognise that social contact and belonging to a group can be helpful in getting the work done, especially in relieving a tedious task.

Maslow's next level, esteem needs, have traditionally been met at work through all sorts of status distinctions, for example size of office, company car, having a secretary, etc. Most organisations have not dramatically reduced these distinctions by, for example, everyone having the same holiday entitlement or allowable expenses. This is usually to reduce the number of spurious symbols of esteem rather than to remove symbols of esteem altogether. In fact, it is hard to find an organisation — even a thoroughly heterarchical one — where status is not accorded implicit recognition.

The top of Maslow's hierarchy is self-actualisation. This term is applied to a person who is motivated by the urge to become everything they have the potential to become. This view has been very influential in work organisations as management consultants, organisation developers and advisers on change have pursued these ideals. There is some individual variation in the degree to which self-actualisation can be a motivator. First, it is a learned, culturally determined, need. Second, the other needs must be satisfied first.

Maslow's model is a general model of human motivation. How well suited is Maslow's hierarchy in the work situation? Although it was not devised for looking at motivation at work it has become very popular. It is useful as an indicator of individual differences. Its main strength is in listing what might motivate people. Steers and Porter, in their book *Motivation and Work Behaviour*, suggest various organisational factors which could be used to satisfy different needs.

- Physiological:
  - pay
  - pleasant work conditions
  - dining facilities
- Safety:
  - Health and Safety well monitored
  - company benefits
  - job security
- Social:
  - cohesive work group
  - friendly supervision
  - professional associations
- Esteem:
  - social recognition
  - job title
  - high status job
  - feedback from job itself
- Self-actualisation:
  - challenging job
  - opportunities for creativity
  - achievement in work
  - advancement in the organisation.

The difficulty with using a Maslow approach to motivation at work is that many people will not wish to satisfy all their motivations at work. This implies that the motivating factors at work will not be equal for different people, even where they apparently have the same motives.

Once again, we can see generational differences at work. In *Towards the Third Modernity*, Alain de Vulpian pinpoints the moment in different western societies when the preoccupation with status and standing (accompanied by mass consumerism) switched to a preoccupation with self-development and self-actualisation (accompanied by a rejection of many of the ideas associated with a mass-consumption society). Increasingly, employers need to take these differences into account as they structure reward and recognition packages.

Generational changes in job expectations are increasingly being discussed by commentators on the work habits and preferences of Generation Y employees (those born after 1980). This group tends to prioritise exciting, challenging and flexible work. A detailed analysis of their preferences can be found in results of a survey conducted by the Talentsmoothie group and published as *Generation Y: What they want from work.*

Herzberg's Theory of Motivation at Work

Frederick Herzberg developed Maslow's model with particular reference to people at work. He described the lower order needs as the need for those factors which have the potential to dissatisfy if they are not present but, once the need is met, will not increase motivation by being supplied in greater quantity. These he called the hygiene factors — if managers do not get them right there will be complaints and people will be demotivated; if they are right no one will comment or notice, just like the effect of hygiene in the kitchen. In contrast to the hygiene factors are the satisfiers. People will work for these and want more of them. These satisfiers tend to be intrinsic to the person. The list of satisfiers is more culturally determined than the hygiene factors, so your group may have slightly different ones to those listed in Figure 2. Herzberg's model has been particularly useful in drawing attention to the way jobs are designed so that they are enriched and the quality of life at work can be improved.

FIGURE 2
HERZBERG'S THEORY OF MOTIVATION

Hygiene factors

- Company policy and administration
- Supervision
- Working conditions
- Salary
- Relationship with peers
- Personal life
- Relationship with subordinates
- Status
- Security

Satisfiers

- Achievement
- Recognition
- Work itself
- Responsibility
- Advancement
- Growth

Some of these findings about motivation can be seen in modern concerns about what makes people contribute their best at work. For example, one survey, using the phrases "psychological safety" and "meaningfulness" which are similar, although not identical, to Herzberg's hygiene factors and satisfiers, found that the following job features are said to make people work hard:

- Psychological safety:
  - — Support: authority and backed by boss.
  - — Role clarity: what is expected and to what standard.
  - — Recognition: praise.
- Meaningfulness:
  - — Self-expression: express self.
  - — Contribution: make a difference.
  - — Challenge: feel stretched.

PEOPLE WANT DIFFERENT THINGS AT DIFFERENT TIMES

There are several other important questions about work and people's motivation such as: what is the meaning of work for individuals? Does work have the same importance for us all? Clearly not. Is there some inevitable connection between certain work conditions and experiences and particular attitudes and feelings? What do we mean by job satisfaction? Is it the same for us all?

It is clear that the technology used by workers will constrain the way in which their work can be organised. Whether a work process is done sequentially with everyone adding their little bit or whether each individual can do the whole task will influence how work is organised. The sheer physical scale of an operation and the noise generated whilst doing so will influence how things are organised. The extent to which technological change is continually altering the nature of the work will determine how things are organised. All of these in turn will influence the attitude and behaviour of the workers. For example, some technologies, like printing, allow social groupings at work. Others, such as car assembly, are much more difficult to organise in social groups at a reasonable cost. Some tasks, such as shutting down oil wells, are by definition always happening somewhere different from the previous occasion. Workers engaged in these different tasks will usually have different attitudes and behaviours as a group from groups engaged in the other activities.

One classic study, which introduced the concept of "orientation to work", examined the attitude and behaviour of assembly line workers at the Vauxhall plant in the UK. They found that different workers had different wants and expectations of work; that is, work had a different meaning for them. They distinguished three main orientations to work:

- An "instrumental" approach to work meant work is a means to an end outside the work situation. Work is a means of acquiring the income to support a valued way of life.
- A "bureaucratic" orientation describes people who sought to give services to a company over a long time in return for a career that saw some promotion and increases in salary, security and pay.
- A "solidaristic orientation" characterised those people who in addition to an economic orientation to work also valued group loyalty to their mates.

This research work suggests that not everyone is seeking self-actualisation through work; maybe they are resigned to being unable to do so. It is a useful counterpoint to the assumptions made by Maslow and Herzberg. Discussing the meaning of, and attitude to, work involves our basic assumptions about morals, power, equality, the rights of individuals and so on, all of which have a political aspect to them.

Force Field Theory

Another theory which adds an important dimension to the models of Maslow and Herzberg is the *force field theory* of Kurt Lewin. Lewin emphasises that individuals operate in a field of forces that represent subjective perceptions about the environment, the importance of a goal and the psychological distance of the goal. Lewin uses it to try to account for the difference of motivation in people at different times. For example, you and I might both want to meet the boss. I see the circumstances as far too difficult; the goal of seeing the boss is not compelling enough to overcome the psychological distance and make any effort to see them worthwhile. You, however, may be in more favourable circumstances, may want to see the boss enough to overcome the psychological distance between you. So you will be more motivated to try and meet the boss than I am.

Goal Theory

A similar theory of motivation to work is *goal theory*, based on the work of Edwin Locke. The basic premise of goal theory is that people's goals or intentions play an important part in determining behaviour. This relates to the perceived value of expectancy theories. People strive to achieve goals in order to satisfy their emotions and desires. The goals guide people's responses and actions which at work will affect their work behaviour and performance. In management circles this theory is related to the Management by Objectives (MBO) approach to performance management, although MBO was devised before the development of goal theory. If appropriate goals are set for people they are more likely to be motivated to achieve them, as they know what is expected.

Expectancy Theory

An additional view about motivation is called *expectancy theory*. This is the influence on our motivation of our expectancy of the success of our actions. The more likely we think it is that we will be successful the more effort we will put in, and vice versa. For example, if I feel that when I go to the meeting I will be able to contribute I am more likely to put the effort into going than if I expect to find that I am not listened to. My expectancy of success influences my motivation to go to the meeting. Another concept that Victor Vroom uses in relation to expectancy theory is "valence", which is the degree of preference an individual attaches to a particular outcome; this can be positive, negative or indifferent. This is where you might prefer to influence people at the meeting and so are motivated to put the effort in, whereas I am not motivated by the outcome of the meeting so attach a negative "valence" and show little motivation to attend the meeting. The theory then makes the motivation of the individual a result of expectancy and the valence attached to the outcome, or the equation M=ExV.

One influence on expectancy is the perceived equitability of the results. This is people's feelings about how fairly treated they have been in comparison with others. This is based on exchange theory where people expect certain outcomes in exchange for certain contributions. For example, if in meetings two of us are always contributing to the discussion and have always done the preparation when the others have not we may begin to feel very demotivated and begin to make less effort.

There Are Cultural Differences in What Motivates

There seems little doubt that beyond the very basic needs of food, shelter and safety our wants are culturally determined. For example in western cultures we tend to emphasise individuality and achievement, whereas in many eastern cultures there is an emphasis on the family and group achievements, and fitting in and being accepted is valued highly. These affect what people are motivated to work for. How stable these culturally determined motivations are, how varied and whether they can be influenced is the subject of much academic debate and really too theoretical for our needs here.

Summary Checklist

1. People want, that is they are motivated by, different things.
2. People have different attitudes to work.
3. There is a hierarchy of physiological, safety, social, esteem and self-actualisation needs.
4. The first two of these can be seen as hygiene factors whereas the last three are satisfiers.
5. All motivation depends on the situation.
6. Motivation is affected by the importance we attach to particular goals, the perceived likelihood of achieving them, the fairness of the situation and our particular value systems and beliefs.
7. There are cultural and generational differences in the higher order needs.

Part 2

How Do We Win and Retain Employee Motivation and Commitment?

EMPLOYEE MOTIVATION AUDIT AND SCORING SYSTEM

The rest of this audit is based on steps. Each step is a description of the sorts of things organisations can do to increase employee motivation and commitment at work. Each step of the employee motivation audit contains a self-assessment audit to measure whether an organisation has the factors that engender employee commitment associated with effectiveness. This is best done by line managers, senior management and personnel or human resources managers. You as an organisation need to decide the scale of the audit. You may wish to do it in a part of the organisation where there is a problem or make it a general audit after a major change. Clearly the larger the audit the more resources will be involved. It can also be a useful starting point for an away-day for senior managers, team leaders or teams to get them talking about how they really motivate the people in their teams.

When you have done the appropriate audit you may identify a problem area where there is a difference between what is needed and what is the reality. You then need to look further at how to develop commitment in that area. On the whole it should be obvious where to start once you have identified the problem. If not, you may find guidance and more detail in the companion HR audits from Cambridge Strategy Publications.

The audit lists several factors contributing to the effectiveness of each step. Each factor should be given a rating of 1 to 6, and 7 should be done by the self-assessor. Rating 1 is the least involved and 6 the most involved using the following criteria. Rating 7 is an overall assessment of whether you have achieved what you set out to do.

1. No knowledge of the factor
2. Only a conceptual awareness of the factor
3. No need for this in our organisation
4. Some need for this, less than 50 per cent implementation in our organisation
5. Need for this factor in 50 to 80 per cent of our organisation
6. Need for this throughout our organisation
7. We have achieved this factor to the level desired in our organisation.

As with all aspects of organisational behaviour, there are no right answers.

Step 1

Do We Consider What Will Motivate Our Employees Individually?

This introductory step is to ensure that the organisation considers people as individuals and does not treat everyone the same. Formally this is done through job descriptions, appraisal schemes and reward systems. Each person will end up with at least a slightly different outcome. These are dealt with in more detail later. Informally we treat people individually in our conversations, our reactions to them and the flexibility in the way we work with each other. These are also dealt with later.

Step 1 of this audit is to ensure that as an organisation you take into account individual differences and ensure that there is a range of rewards available for people at work. The following audit questions use material from Part One for you to apply to your organisation. The scoring system, which is the same for each series of questions, is explained in the previous section.

Step 1 Audit

	Rating						
	1	2	3	4	5	6	7
1. We find out what individuals want from work							
2. We take into account individual differences in motivation at work							
3. We ensure and monitor that the basic needs of our employees at work are met and suitable							
4. We provide opportunities for people to meet their social and esteem needs at work							
5. We provide the opportunity for meaningful work							
6. We find out what different motivation different groups of our employees have, and provide for this.							

Step 2

WHAT SORTS OF REWARD AND RECOGNITION PROGRAMMES DO WE RUN?

Understanding what motivates people at work will also suggest appropriate rewards for them in response to their contribution. Although reward management is a study in itself, see Michael Armstrong's book *Employee Reward*, some understanding of the different rewards to be used can suggest different ways an organisation might approach individuals. They include:

- pay:
  - for time
  - by results
  - for merit
  - performance related
  - share ownership
  - profit related
- other benefits:
  - pensions
  - sick pay
  - insurance schemes and other financial benefits
- work/task:
  - variety of work and skills used
  - autonomy and involvement
- social/people:
  - interactions with others
  - recognition and feedback.

The nature of the rewards can influence a number of areas of employee behaviour and commitment which in turn affect the organisation's performance.

- Rewards influence who is attracted to apply and work for the organisation. High wages attract more applicants and they are more likely to stay. High performers are attracted by performance related schemes.
- Reward systems signal the importance employers place on various behaviours. Where performance related pay is only on annual targets then short-term objectives are looked after, but the longer-term sustainability of the organisation may be threatened.

- What is rewarded will affect the organisational culture. For example if long service is rewarded, loyalty to the organisation will be central, whereas if innovation is rewarded a more dynamic culture will develop.

- Reward systems can support a status difference and influence who is responsible for decisions. Organisations differ widely in the ratio of the highest to lowest paid member. Where there is a wide ratio difference, say 30:1 with the highest paid person being paid thirty times as much as the lowest, there is less likely to be equal motivation to contribute to decision-making than in an organisation with a narrower ratio.

- As discussed in the previous section, individuals with different goals and work preferences will be motivated by different kinds of reward. Generational differences also play a part here. Organisations need to develop flexibility and variety in their reward schemes to ensure that, for example, they can attract young salespeople, experienced creative people and career-minded financial executives.

When considering the strategic design of reward systems Edward Lawler suggests there are a number of questions to consider.

- Basis of rewards:
  - are people paid for the jobs they do or for the competencies they have? The latter leads to a more flexible workforce.

- Pay for performance or seniority:
  - performance related pay has its problems, so should you consider motivation through other means such as personal growth and recognition?

- Market position:
  - do you want to be seen as a market leader and part of the elite?

- Internal or external pay comparisons:
  - for large conglomerates and multinationals particularly the question is whether everyone working for the organisation, whatever the business, wherever it is, should be treated similarly or whether there should be comparison with similar industries and locations.

- Communication policy:
  - how open or closed the organisation is about rewards depends on its philosophy.

- Decision-making practices:
  - who is involved in making decisions about the reward system? Employees, employee representatives and line managers all change the nature of the legitimacy of the system in the eye of employees.

There is no right or wrong answer to these. It is more a case of choosing a system that supports the nature of the organisation that will deliver the desired performance.

That is the reward systems need to support the managerial philosophy and business strategy. See *The Reward and Benefits Audit* in this series for further detail.

Summary Checklist

1. Pay and rewards affect the organisation performance as they tell people what is valued and rewarded.
2. Pay and rewards signal what is seen as important in the particular organisation which in turn will affect the organisational culture.
3. Pay and rewards also affect who is motivated to join and who stays with the organisation.
4. It is important to make the reward system fit in with the desired nature of the organisation.

Step 2 Audit

	Rating						
	1	2	3	4	5	6	7
1. Our reward system rewards the competencies of individuals.							
2. Our pay scheme rewards performance.							
3. We position ourselves at the top of the market for pay.							
4. We pay everyone in our organisation on the same basis.							
5. We operate an open communication policy about reward systems.							
6. We involve as wide a range of staff as possible in designing our pay schemes.							

Step 3

Is the Work Organised so that It Can Be Motivating For People?

Non-financial rewards and recognition are also important in motivating people at work. There are a number of different aspects of work that can be motivating. Here are six attributes, first identified by Turner and Lawrence:

- variety — tools, equipment, prescribed workplace
- autonomy — discretion to choose work method
- required interactions — necessary contact with others
- optional interaction — opportunities for contact
- knowledge and skill — learning
- responsibility — such as problem-solving.

J. Richard Hackman develops this a bit further and suggests that there are various dimensions in jobs which are associated with good performance by the job-holder. See Figure 3 where the five characteristics are Hackman's. We might want to add the following based on the human relations models.

- Dealing with others — how much staff have to deal with other people will vary and different amounts suit different people
- Friendship opportunities — establishing informal relationships at work again is of varying importance to different people.

These dimensions give meaning to work, responsibility to the job holders and knowledge of how they are doing. By taking various actions, see Figure 4, motivation and performance can in this model be improved.

As an example of how these characteristics work, many of the ideas have been incorporated in the concept of individual team members having their own customers. For example, in hospitals, patients having a named nurse — not only does the patient know who their carer is but the nurses get some of the above characteristics in their working day.

FIGURE 3 JOB DIMENSIONS AND THEIR AFFECTS	
1. *Skill variety.* The way a job demands a variety of different activities that involve using a number of different skills and talents. 2. *Task identity.* The way a job requires the job-holder to complete a whole and coherent piece of work having a tangible outcome. 3. *Task significance.* The way a job has an impact on the lives or work of other people, inside the organisation or outside.	These give meaning to the work people do.
4. *Autonomy.* The way a job-holder enjoys freedom from supervision, independence and discretion in deciding how the job should be done.	This gives responsibility to job-holders.
5. *Feedback.* The way the job-holder receives clear and direct information about his or her effectiveness.	This gives the job-holder knowledge of results.

Adapted from J.R. Hackman, "Work Design", in *Motivation and Work Behaviour.*

FIGURE 4
WAYS OF GETTING GOOD RESULTS ON THE FIVE JOB DESCRIPTIONS

Action	Job dimension affected
1. *Forming natural work units* so that the work to be done has a logic and makes sense to the job-holder.	2, 3
2. *Combining tasks* so that a number of natural work units may be put together to make a bigger and more coherent job.	1, 2
3. *Establishing links with clients* so that the job-holder has contact with people using the service or product the job-holder is supplying.	1, 4, 5
4. *Vertical loading* so that job-holders take on more of the management of their jobs in deciding what to do, organising their own time, solving their own problems and controlling their own costs.	4
5. *Opening feedback channels* so that job-holders can discover more about how they are doing and whether their performance is improving or deteriorating.	5

Adapted from J.R. Hackman (ibid).

Several different ways of improving job satisfaction, and so motivation, through redesign have been tried. The major ways of redesigning, or designing, jobs are:

- job rotation — moving from one job to another to reduce boredom and increase skills. For example in one chemical factory the operators are moved around from receiving goods from suppliers, to checking the process, running the process, and packing the final product ready for transport to their customers
- job enlargement — increase the number of tasks done by an individual. For example the waiting staff at TGI Fridays, a restaurant chain, are expected to entertain and "host" the customers at their tables. The job is larger than just taking orders, serving meals and clearing dishes
- job enrichment — broaden the responsibilities and increase individual autonomy for decision-making. For example, hotel reception staff can negotiate the price charged for a room that night and work out a suitable package rather than having to keep to a set price and lose the customer
- autonomous work teams — where the team decides how, when and for how much the work is done. This requires a skilled team and needs management to be prepared to let go. It has been most frequently used in the USA and Scandinavia
- leadership models — where the vision of the leader is sufficient to give meaning and significance to everyone, jobs can feel more worthwhile. It is however difficult to achieve most of this (see Step 4)
- quality movement — concentrates on the process of the work rather than the people but assumes people will be challenged by the need for constant improvement
- flexibility — where people work non-traditional hours.

All of these can be used successfully at team, section or departmental level. However, they can also all feel very manipulative if staff are suspicious, feeling aggrieved over pay and conditions or are left feeling uncertain about their personal futures. Like all change it needs careful managing and implementation.

Many of these issues are discussed at greater length by Gerard Fairtlough in *The Three Ways of Getting Things Done*. He highlights the strengths of 'heterarchy' and 'responsible automony' as against the conventional, hierarchical approach to managing work. Note that autonomy, whether applied to work teams or individuals, is a more sophisticated approach to job enrichment than that offered by empowerment. Autonomous working also implies and requires considerable levels of trust within organisations. The question of trust is discussed at greater length by Sally Bibb in her book *Trust Matters* and by Gerard Fairtlough in *No Secrets!*.

The common themes relating to non-financial rewards and motivation are recognition, feedback, involvement, autonomy and responsibility. The art is to do this with a sufficiently light hand not to seem patronising, and to catch staff doing it right, as rewarding good work is more effective than criticising bad work. See *The Organisational Change Audit* in this series for further development of these issues.

Summary Checklist

1. Jobs can be satisfying because of the variety, autonomy, interaction and responsibility the job-holder can experience.
2. Jobs can be satisfying because of the opportunity given for practising technical knowledge and skills.
3. Work can be redesigned to be more motivating for employees by taking into consideration the above factors by job rotation, enlargement, enrichment.
4. Work can be redesigned into work teams, with better leaders.
5. Flexibility of working hours can also gain the commitment of many employees.

Step 3 Audit

	Rating 1	2	3	4	5	6	7
1. We provide our staff with a suitable degree of variety in their jobs.							
2. We provide our staff with meaningful work to do.							
3. There is suitable recognition of each person's contribution at work.							
4. We give individual feedback to members of the organisation.							
5. We include people in decisions about the work they do.							
6. Members of the organisation have some autonomy in what they do at work and how they do it.							
7. People have responsibility to make decisions about the nature of their work.							

Step 4

What is the Effect of Our Leadership Style and Content on Employee Motivation?

To gain employee commitment there are two aspects that need to be considered: content and process. First, is there something for them to do? If so, is it clear what that is, who is going to do it and how? Is there a consensus about what the task is and is this agreed not only by those within the team but by those outside who may overlap or need to coordinate with the team? The second issue that needs to be considered is how the people work together. Are they complementary and aiding each other to get the best out of the team? Are there some processes which are hindering them? Are there some sorts of tasks that the team is better at than others?

To answer these questions about particular individuals or teams we often end up asking questions about how they are managed or led. Questions such as: how much autonomy do they have? How much do they feel as one about what they are doing? What sorts of pressures are on them to conform? The currently preferred term in management circles is "leadership" which, it is claimed, is different from "management" in that it is about enabling others to perform rather than making them perform.

Nowadays you will hear phrases about leadership competencies like:

- maintain the trust and support of colleagues and team members
- set up collaborative and consultative working arrangements
- provide the environment for people to excel
- nurture individual development
- recognise success
- encourage enthusiasm through teamwork.

None of us would disagree with these as worthy ambitions for leaders. But it is quite difficult to see how exactly a team leader should go about achieving them. The two essential tasks of leadership seem to be clarifying the tasks to be done and establishing suitable enthusiasm and expertise in the people to undertake the tasks effectively. However, there are, as ever, several different approaches to analysing leadership and we will look at different approaches in the following sections.

The roles of the leader

After the early studies had failed to come up with any useful personality traits (qualities) that were associated with leaders another more pragmatic approach was to look at what functions a leader fulfils for the group. Various studies looked at the work done by managers and leaders. This sort of research led to a description of the various roles that leaders could or should fill in organisations.

A useful summary by David Krech et al suggests the following possible roles for the leaders.

- Coordinator — of the various functions and work of others
- Planner — to realise the goals of the organisation
- Policy-maker — to work out how we are going to do things
- Expert — in the technology or processes of the organisation
- External group representative — to customers, suppliers and other agencies
- Controller of internal relations — between groups and individuals
- Control of rewards and punishments — salaries, promotions, developments and careers
- Arbitration and mediation — where conflict is unresolved
- Role model — of acceptable behaviour in this organisation
- Symbol of the group — embodying the culture of the organisation
- Ideologist — having a strong articulated mission
- Parent figure — who can always cope with the unexpected and take an interest in individuals
- Scapegoat — someone to blame for the ills of the organisation.

No one is suggesting that every manager or leader plays all these roles but these are typical roles filled by leaders within organisations. The latter roles will influence the motivation of others more than the first roles.

Styles of Leadership

An early influential model of leadership has been that of John Adair. He argued that people working in groups have three sets of needs, two of which are shared with all group members, the third being related to each individual.

- The task to be accomplished together.
- Maintaining social cohesion of the group.
- Individual needs of team members.

These three sets of needs are interdependent. If the task fails there is diminished satisfaction for the individual and the group tends to fall apart. If the group lacks unity this will affect performance. If the individual is discontented then they will not give their best performance. Figure 5 shows these three sets of needs, or leadership functions, as three overlapping circles. This emphasises the essential unity of leadership, so that a single action by a leader may have an influence in all three areas.

FIGURE 5
ADAIR'S THREE CIRCLE MODEL OF LEADERSHIP

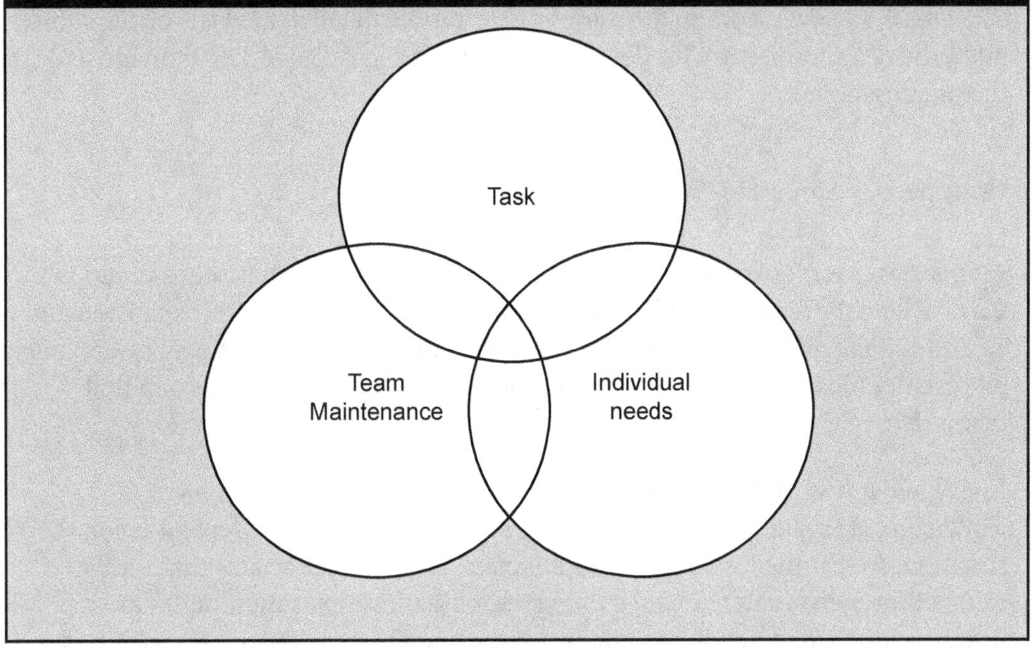

Another well-tried device for identifying leadership style of the individual is Blake and Mouton's managerial grid. This is used as an exercise in finding one's current leadership style with the hope that it can be modified, at least slightly, to become more appropriate to the situation in which one is working. The managerial grid identifies concern for production and concern for people as the two axes of the grid. These result in a grid of different types of leader. For example, at the extremes:

- the style of managers with a low concern for both people and production, who try to stay out of trouble and simply do what they are told
- a style with high concern for people but low concern for production. This is the utterly delightful leader, full of charm and consideration, who never quite gets round to making anything happen
- the person with high concern for production and little concern for people. They are full of ideas on what to get done and what needs doing but are very frustrated when no one pays any attention or they do not get others to cooperate with them
- the style of high concern with both people and production is the obvious goal. These leaders are able to motivate people to make an appropriate contribution with enthusiasm.

This emphasis on style, rather than personal characteristics, is probably the secret of the success that grid methods have enjoyed as it provides useful criticism of the type that most people can live with and hope to modify. This grid could also be used as a way of analysing the general culture or behaviour in organisations and whether the concern for both people and tasks is in balance and whether some changes are required.

The Leadership Skills Audit in this series offers a more detailed analysis of the subject and provides a framework for developing leadership profiles of key individuals within the organisation.

Contingency Models of Leadership

So far we have looked at leadership in various ways but with no consideration of where the leader is performing. Clearly to lead in a period of expansion and wealth is quite different from times of hardship and fear. The contingency approach emphasises the importance of the situation that the leader and the group find themselves in.

Fred Fiedler was the first to use the phrase "contingency" in the context of leadership. He argues that any leadership style may be effective depending on the situation, so that the leader has to be adaptive. He also appreciates that it is very difficult for individuals to change their style of leadership as these styles are relatively inflexible: the autocrat will remain autocratic and the free-wheeling laissez-faire advocate will remain free-wheeling. As no single style is appropriate in all situations, effectiveness can either be achieved by changing the leader to fit the situation or by altering the situation to fit the leader.

Three factors will determine the leader's effectiveness:

- leader-member relations. How well is the leader accepted by the other members?

- task structure. Are the jobs of the members routine and precise or vague and undefined?
- Position power. What formal authority does the leader's position confer?

More recently, Bill Tate (author of *The Organisational Leadership Audit*) has stressed the importance of looking at the overall leadership culture in the organisation, rather than focusing on the skills of particular individuals. His 'ecological' approach to leadership, which strongly emphasises contingency, is more closely in tune with current organisational thinking.

The Drive for Leadership in Organisations

John Kotter saw management as predominantly activity-based whereas leadership means dealing with people rather than things. Management involves the following.

- Planning and budgeting. This involves target-setting; establishing procedures for reaching targets; allocating the resources necessary to meet plans.
- Organising and staffing. This is setting the organisation structure. It means recruiting the right people and giving them incentives.
- Controlling and problem-solving. This means monitoring the results compared with the plan. It involves identifying problems and working out solutions.

Everything is concerned with logic, structure, analysis and control and if well done it produces predictable results on time. Leadership on the other hand is:

- creating a sense of direction. This is usually as a result of dissatisfaction with the status quo. It is challenged. Out of this challenge a vision for something different is born
- communicating the vision. The vision must be the realised or unconscious needs of other people and the leader must work to give it credibility
- energising, inspiring and motivating. These words encapsulate much of what a leader must be seen to do. People must be kept moving, enthusiasm must be bred and maintained and when the going is tough they must be supported and helped.

If done well, and with passion and commitment, then it will produce impetus for change. If no change is necessary, frankly management might be better! Where change is necessary, management will be found lacking and the need for leadership will be paramount.

In management circles, Human Resource Management circles in particular, there is presently a great deal of emphasis on developing leadership in those with responsibilities for managing people. They speak of moving from management to leadership. The factor prompting this move is an ideal of moving from compliance to commitment, based on the humanistic approach of many working in this field. There is also a feeling that as organisations become less hierarchical and more team and project based, individuals will belong to several teams and will be required to offer their contribution rather than have it demanded of them.

Mobilising this commitment through effective leadership has become one of the recent buzz terms of management. There is a particular emphasis on the visionary constituents of leadership and the ability to inspire others through a suitable statement of the purpose and mission of the group. Words about how people can be taken out of themselves and achieve more than they imagined are often bandied about. It remains to be seen whether this will work, and whether criteria for effective leadership behaviour can be distinguished. It is also worth remembering that leaders can only lead as far as followers allow them unless some coercion is involved.

A popular distinction between leaders is that made between transactional and transformational leaders.

- Transactional leaders use styles of communication and techniques to clarify task requirements and ensure that there are appropriate rewards when the task is completed. Sometimes called command and control type leadership.
- Transformational leaders are those who articulate a mission and create and maintain a positive image in followers and superiors. These are sometimes called visionary leaders.

The latter sort of leader, with its emphasis on motivating others to achieve, has become the more accepted definition of what leadership is about.

The Control-Participation Dilemma

There is some confusion about leadership and empowerment (see Step 6) because of the aspects of power, authority and control implicit in the relationship of leader and led. The control-participation dilemma shows the interdependence of the leader and the led and the balance of power between them. Compliance or commitment is the result.

A useful model is that of Tannenbaum and Schmidt who suggest a continuum of behaviour by leaders and those who work for them. The continuum is:

- at one end the leader makes all the decisions and announces them
- the leader sells the decision
- the leader presents ideas and invites questions
- the leader presents tentative decisions subject to change
- the leader presents problems and gets suggestions and makes the decision

- the leader defines the limits and asks the group to make the decision
- at the other end the leader permits the group to function within limits defined by others.

Moving along this continuum it is about the amount of control that the leader has over the led. It is also about the level of participation of the led. This has led to the use of four words to define these different sorts of leaders:

- tells
- sells
- consults
- joins.

This brief summary is often used informally in organisations to describe a boss's behaviour. It simply describes the move from compliance to commitment.

Criteria for Effective Leadership

So how do we judge who are and who can be effective leaders? Several lists of generic management competencies look very much like leadership competencies. For example the MCI (Management Charter Initiative, which is the NVQ body for management standards in the UK) list includes such phrases as:

- establish organisational values and culture
- inspire people
- establish integrity and ethics
- communicate sensitively.

These competencies can only be judged by seeing people in action.

Credibility

Credibility is the word used in organisations, particularly amongst professionals, to describe the prerequisite ability that you need in order to get things done. In the increasingly informal working of organisations this credibility is something you have to earn and maintain for yourself. The job title and organisational position will help but will not be sufficient. Those with high credibility are worthy of belief, trustworthy, convincing and respected. They are listened to and can get things done willingly and quickly, whereas colleagues who lack credibility meet resistance and have to rely more heavily on the glacial speed of formal mechanisms.

The basis of credibility is usually an appropriate expertise and some contribution of personal qualities such as hard work and enthusiasm. It is a very rare individual who can rely on personal attributes alone to be credible. Leadership is more often made up of hard work, understanding of the position and position power. The components of a leader's credibility might be:

- keeping in touch with the main task — it is only by keeping in touch with the main task of the organisation as a whole and the section in which the leader is located that new ideas can be based in reality. If they lose touch with their operational expertise they risk losing credibility with their colleagues. Staff can become sceptical about how much they understand current operational problems and the manager will retreat further into management and administration. This in turn creates unnecessary and superfluous systems of control that infuriate the staff

- legitimacy — staff on the receiving end of managers exercising authority respond readily only when they perceive the authority as legitimate. The formal organisation charts, job titles and pay structures provide those in authority with legitimacy. Western society and its organisations have developed a taste for informal means to supplement these. Keeping in touch with the main task and maintaining technical competence is the main feature but authority is also legitimised by such personal characteristics as willingness to do things, working hard and demonstrating enthusiasm. Belonging to the organisation and being seen to be committed to it can be crucial in being able to influence things. Experience enables some people to develop a "nose" for appropriate times and actions. They have invaluable legitimacy. The fact that this cannot be learned does not reduce its importance

- a clear role — it has been found that many managerial jobs do not have any clear role. People with these jobs are not in charge of anything and consequently the individuals, who are often hard-working, experienced and keen, will find work to do. Not all of this is helpful as it often interferes with other people's work, particularly where the work created is predominantly administrative and increases the amount of administration done by those required to respond.

When deadlines are tight and the pressure is on, credible leaders can get away with some brusqueness to get things done where others will not. But this should be the exception if leaders are doing their job right and want to maintain credibility and the commitment of their teams.

The characteristics which undermine credibility are: appearing to do useless things, adding to the burden of others unnecessarily and bandwagoning for personal gain. But different cultures and organisations will reflect different things, so any particular organisation may well have other behaviours that add to or subtract from credibility.

The important thing is to know the basis of your credibility and work on maintaining it.

The consequences of not having credibility are that those working with you will be frustrated and less compliant, peers will take you less seriously, bosses may only include you as a back-up to themselves, and customers, clients, and others outside the organisation may come to devalue the whole organisation.

Just as important as acquiring credibility is the process of maintaining credibility. It is no use relying on expertise and practical experience gained five or ten years ago. No young member of staff will be impressed with "well, we used to do it like this and it was fine" or " fifteen years ago we had the same problem and I managed to fix it". Far better to offer the advice as current and try to encourage a mutual problem-solving approach.

Leadership is important for employee motivation as the leader affects what is done and how it gets done. Working for a leader who inspires confidence and is credible can increase motivation and commitment. A leader who frustrates and lacks credibility undermines the confidence and commitment of the led. The main aspect of leadership that affects employee motivation is that the leadership is seen as credible by those being led and that it is seen as appropriate to the task in hand. No amount of communication about the wonders of senior management will impress employees if they see the leaders as being out of touch.

Summary Checklist

1. Management is about dealing with activities; leadership is more people-centred.

2. There are different possible roles for leaders as:
— coordinator, planner, policy-maker, expert, external relations, controller, arbitrator, role model, symbol, ideologist, parent figure and scapegoat.

3. It appears that different leadership styles are suitable to different situations.

4. There are transactional and transformational leaders.

5. A difference between leaders is that some tell, others sell, others consult and some join.

6. Leaders need to be credible with the led, and the easiest way to ensure this is to keep in touch with what is going on.

Step 4 Audit

	Rating						
	1	2	3	4	5	6	7
1. We have leaders not managers.							
2. Our leaders give clear indications of what we want achieved.							
3. Our leaders are focused on people more than activities.							
4. The role of our leaders is to enable others to perform.							
5. We have a variety of leaders to suit different situations.							
6. Our leaders are credible.							

Step 5

Do We Build Effective Teams that Assist in Gaining Employee Commitment?

One popular metaphor about teams is to compare them with geese flying in a V shape. Geese manage to migrate long distances by taking it in turn to lead the V, so allowing the others to fly in their slipstream, each subsequent goose helping the one behind. By all helping and contributing the whole skein of geese get further than any one of them could have managed on their own. The importance of belonging to such a team so that everyone achieves more and consequently is more motivated is part of the current emphasis on teams at work. This is not just a romantic idea but one based on research.

Buchanan and Huczynski suggest that groups, whether formal or informal, have the following structure regarding how they relate to each other.

- Status
- Power
- Roles
- Leadership
- Communication.

If you can analyse, describe and understand these aspects of the team you appreciate the nature of their behaviour.

Group Theory

There is an important distinction made in the analysis of groups or teams between content and process. Content is concerned with what groups do, the task they set themselves and why they are doing something. The process of the group is how they do things and how they interact with each other. Figure 6 lists various attributes of this process and content. Details are given of two important aspects of teams for developing commitment but for further information see any book on organisational behaviour, such as Laurie Mullins' *Management and Organisational Behaviour*.

FIGURE 6
FACTORS INFLUENCING TEAM BEHAVIOUR AND PERFORMANCE

Process	Content
Team dynamics	**Team purpose**
Cohesion Interaction Norms Stability	Nature of task Reasons for team
TEAM	
Team organisation	**Team environment**
Size Membership Leadership Communication Roles	Physical External threat Social context Body language Technology

Team cohesion

Bruce Tuckman suggests that there are various stages small groups go through before they are mature enough in their relations to be able to work together consistently. These stages are set out in Figure 7. These stages are helpful in showing that team development takes time to become effective. This time will vary according to how long the team is going to work together. It may take several months for a long-term group because the degree of commitment required from each member is high and the risk of personal failure so great. Whereas in the short-term, part-time group the risk is lower and the tolerance higher. So when your work team is going through an argumentative period you might consider whether this is a stage in developing group cohesion or is happening for some other reason. Another time to use this model is when setting up a new team and needing to expect some variation in the emotional climate of the team.

See Andrew Carey's *Project Red Stripe* for a detailed analysis of this approach in relation to an innovation project team at *The Economist*.

Team roles

Meredith Belbin looked at the different roles that are necessary for management teams to be effective. He identified eight:

- the *company worker* who works to keep the organisation's interests to the fore
- the *chair* who ensures that all views are heard and keeps things moving
- the *shaper* who influences by argument and by following particular topics

FIGURE 7
STAGES IN THE GROWTH OF GROUP COHESION AND PERFORMANCE

Stage of development	*Process*	*Outcome*
1. Forming	There is anxiety, dependence on leader; testing to find out the nature of the situation and what behaviour is acceptable	Members find out what the taskis, what the rules are and whatmethods are appropriate
2. Storming	Conflict between sub-groups, rebellion against leader; opinions are polarised; resistance to control by group	Emotional resistance to demands of task
3. Norming	Development of group cohesion; norms emerge; resistance is overcome and conflicts are patched up; mutual support and sense of group identity	Open exchange of views and feelings; cooperation develops
4. Performing	Interpersonal problems are resolved; interpersonal structure becomes the means of getting things done; roles are flexible and functional	Solutions to problems emerge; there are constructive attempts to complete tasks and energy is now available for effective work

Based on B. W. Tuckman, "Development Sequences in Small Groups".

- the *ideas* person or plant who contributes novel suggestions
- the *resource investigator* who evaluates whether contributions are practical and finds out where and how to obtain resources
- the *monitor/evaluator* who assesses how valid the contributions are
- the *team worker* who maintains the group by joking and agreeing
- the *completer/finisher* who tries to get things done and suggests conclusions.

At different times, each of these roles needs filling for teams to work effectively. Most of us fill more than one. Again the main use of this model is to emphasise that different contributions are required to keep things moving in a group.

Maureen Guirdham offers the following characteristics of a fully effective team.

- Team objectives are clearly understood by all members.
- All members are committed to the objectives.
- Mutual trust is high.
- Support for one another is high.
- Communications are open and reliable, not guarded and cautious.

- Team members listen to one another, understanding and being understood.
- The team is self controlling.
- Conflicts are accepted and worked through.
- Members' abilities, knowledge and experience are fully used by the team.

Most of these characteristics concentrate on the process side of groups working. That is the way people work together. It is also important to look at the *content* — what the group has to do. Guirdham emphasises this by putting it first. Effective teams have both a good task orientation and a cohesion amongst the group. The expressions "process" and "content" are important terms for analysing teams and are worth keeping in mind if you find yourself in an ineffective team, group or meeting. Is the problem a content one, that is an unclear or impossible objective, or is it a process problem, that is the group is not working well together for this sort of task? The reason many team-building exercises are carried out outdoors is because the objective is clear and it is clear what the result is. This makes the analysis of the process, the purpose of the exercise, clearer than would endless debates about what the goal was and whether it was achieved.

The Disadvantages of Teams

Throughout this step there has been an emphasis on the effectiveness of teams and how best to enhance this. There are however some difficulties with emphasising group or team work.

Individuals

Not everything is best done by a group despite the current emphasis on teams. Some things need to be done by individuals and it is counterproductive to get a team involved. Even some decisions are best made singly. Although you then do not have the commitment of anyone else to putting that decision into practice.

Conflict

Although competition in the market-place is at the very heart of capitalism, competition in the workplace can be a waste. Competitiveness in the organisation usually results in energy being expended at the expense of the overall aims and objectives of the organisation. But some competitiveness is encouraged by employers when they feel that competing teams will egg each other on to greater sales. For example many sales teams compete for monthly prizes. Like so many things in organisations it all comes down to a balance between extremes. The term coopetition has been coined to describe the use of cooperative competition in this context.

Groupthink

Irving Janis studied the decision-making of the United States foreign policy groups. He found that a cohesive group of individuals, sharing a common fate, exerts a strong pressure towards conformity. He found that President Kennedy's "Bay of Pigs" fiasco in the early 1960s, where the USA and Russia came close to war over the placing of missiles in Cuba, and the disaster in Vietnam in the 1960s and 1970s, where the USA was fighting the local communists of North Vietnam, could not be accounted for by individual incompetence. He coined the term "groupthink" to cover the exaggeration of irrational tendencies that seems to occur in groups. He argues that the group setting can magnify weaknesses of judgement.

This groupthink concept is perhaps most useful as a warning that teams are not always a good thing. For example when change is being proposed there is a tendency to dismiss those who are reluctant to support the innovation as dull, unimaginative, obstinate or behind the times. This may be so but it is sometimes the case that the proposed change is not so good after all and the rest were suffering from some sort of groupthink.

Developing effective teams is important for employee motivation as so much of our work has to be done in groups or teams to get the work done. How well we work together will affect our feelings of usefulness and cohesion, both of which are strong motivators. Teams are also effective ways of meeting some of the basic social needs of belonging and esteem. This enthusiasm for teams needs balancing with meeting our individual needs as well. This balancing act between the needs of the individual and the needs of the group is one of Adair's challenges for leaders, as we saw in the previous step. Motivating teams is an important part of leadership which was also dealt with in the previous step. See The Teams Audit in this series for further information.

Summary Checklist

1. Teams have status, power, roles, leaders and communication needs.

2. We can distinguish the following attributes in teams:
   - on the process side — dynamics and organisation.
   - on the content side — purpose and environment.

3. Team cohesion develops through several stages.

4. There are several roles that need taking for a team to be effective.

5. Effective teams have a high level of trust.

6. The disadvantages of teams are the expense of time, conflict and groupthink.

Step 5 Audit

	Rating 1	2	3	4	5	6	7
1. We ensure that team objectives are clearly understood by all members.							
2. All members are committed to the objectives.							
3. The level of mutual trust in our teams is high.							
4. The support for one another in teams is high.							
5. In teams communications are open and reliable, not guarded and cautious.							
6. Team members listen to one another, understanding and being understood.							
7. The teams are self controlling.							
8. Conflicts in teams are accepted and worked through.							
9. Members' abilities, knowledge and experience are fully used by the teams.							

Step 6

Do We Involve and Empower Our Employees?

As we saw earlier one of the recurring findings about employee motivation is the effectiveness of involvement and feedback in gaining commitment at work. Indeed the very popularity of the terms "empowerment" and "autonomy" in organisations shows the importance of this. Power is a property that exists in any organisation or system; politics is the way that power is put into action. Those who understand the subtleties of power in relationships are better able to get things done than those who ignore them.

Organisations have power as one of their crucial dimensions, and only by understanding how power is distributed and deployed can members get things done. The innovative idea or accurate diagnosis is insufficient without the means for their implementation. The analysis of power is an important part of understanding how groups work, how leadership is exercised and how commitment from others is achieved.

Jeffrey Pfeffer specifically looked at power in organisations. He suggests that the following elements produce conflict and the use of power in organisations.

- Interdependence — where what happens to one person affects another, such as joint activities. My work affects your work.
- Inconsistent goals — where there are different aims. My aim might conflict with what you are trying to do.
- Technologies — differences will lead to conflict. For example, if you have one IT system and I have another, who should pay to make them compatible? Incidentally this is often an underestimated cost of joint ventures and amalgamation of organisations.
- Scarcity of resources — the greater the scarcity compared with demand the more power and effort will be put into resolving the issue. If we both want to use the piece of equipment we will spend time trying to resolve a suitable rota of use.

All organisations have limited resources for their members so we compete with each other for promotion and career development. On an everyday level we will be competing for a bigger budget, more space, newer equipment, more staff and a greater say over the direction of organisational policy. This competition causes the nature of political activity to vary according to the state of growth or decline of the organisation. With growth there is more opportunity for individuals than in a stagnant state so the organisation is likely to have more winners in a state of growth than in periods of stability or stagnation. So how can power best be distributed to ensure the motivation and commitment of employees?

Power and Control in Organisations

In the past, management was seen as having to control what happened in the organisation by carefully controlling the minute detail of each individual worker. More recently the management approach is to encourage staff to take more power and responsibility for the details of their jobs. There is still central management control of budgets and objectives but less over how to achieve the desired results. Many theories of organisation structure are also theories about who should control what. Power is the extent of real influence that people have in the organisation.

Amitai Etzioni compared a wide range of complex organisations and classified the nature of relationships within them, based on the differences in power and involvement. Members of organisations differed in the way in which they complied with power.

- Coercive power relied on threats, sanctions and force — such as food and comfort.
- Remunerative power involved manipulating rewards such as wages.
- Normative power relied on manipulating symbolic rewards such as esteem and prestige.

Members of organisations varied in their degree of commitment and involvement.

- Alienative involvement is when individuals are there against their wishes.
- Calculative involvement is where attachment is because of extrinsic rewards such as cash.
- Moral involvement is where individuals believe in the goals of the organisation.

Etzioni suggests that a particular kind of power usually goes with a particular kind of involvement.

- Coercive power with alienative involvement; for example in prisons.
- Remunerative power with calculative involvement; for example in many businesses and manufacturing.
- Normative power with moral involvement; for example, charities and religious organisations, and organisations like The Body Shop.

Etzioni suggests that organisations which have matching power and involvement structures are more effective than those that are mismatched. This may account for some organisations' difficulty in implementing the current fashion for empowerment and facilitation. They may really be command and control organisations beneath the apparent new management style.

Empowerment and Autonomy

This simple idea means that employees at all levels are responsible for their actions and should be given the authority to make decisions about their own work. This is not just to make people more satisfied with their work but is done to enable organisations to respond quickly. The advantages claimed for an empowered, autonomous workforce are better services, flexibility, speed, cross-department links, improved morale and compensation for limited career paths. Giving employees the chance to shape their work is not just to make them happier. It has genuine benefits for the organisation as they are generally closer to the customer; they know the customer's needs better than their managers and so often have good ideas about what to do.

Empowerment and autonomy are about ownership of the problem and the solution. True empowerment means employees having the discretion to take decisions about what they feel it is appropriate to do at the time. This empowerment, presumably, also includes the right to be consulted about the nature of the empowerment proposed and indeed the power to say no to empowerment and autonomy.

Typical elements of a system to ensure the success of an empowered, autonomous workforce, from a management perspective, include:

- performance evaluations drawn from a variety of sources
- variable rewards, including some group element
- tolerance of errors
- enhanced communication
- generalist managers and staff
- giving yourself time to develop the confidence in each other
- sufficient resources to deliver some of the solutions that are generated.

Empowerment and responsible autonomy can really only happen where there are sufficient resources to take on any training that is necessary for individuals. Too often empowerment procedures are initiated as a substitute for sufficient resources to get on with the job. It also requires roles to be clearly defined and for the previous managers to give up some of their power.

It is worth thinking about what is in it for each empowered person. This could include such things as:

- a team bonus
- increased recognition
- security of employment
- the satisfaction of developing new talents.

Very often claims to have empowered the staff or achieved responsible autonomy fall well short of these ideals. The difficulties with empowerment from the organisation's point of view are a greater potential for chaos, a lack of clarity, breakdown of hierarchical control and demoralisation of those staff who do not want more responsibility. But without there being something in it for the staff they will feel very put upon, the whole initiative will sink in a flurry of accusations about the latest fashion and fad and it will not work. Empowerment should not feel like dumping! As Hyman and Cunningham found in their research on empowerment in several UK organisations:

> *empowerment in many cases is little different from earlier prescriptions for job enlargement, or at best job enrichment, where employees can exercise discretion and influence over the execution of their immediate tasks, but the overall parameters within which they operate are in many cases not so flexible.*

Equally, Gerard Fairtlough developed the idea of Triarchy Theory to recognise the need for a balance of hierarchy, heterarchy and responsible autonomy. Though he argues that the hegemony of hierarchy is profoundly damaging to organisational effectiveness, he is clear that it needs to be included in the overall mix.

Valuing: Consideration, feedback, Delegation and Participation

If staff are to work so that they willingly contribute their efforts and commitment there has to be something in it for them. Clearly the salary and interest of the work are important parts of this. But where extraordinary commitment is given there is usually something more. This may be because the work itself is seen to matter, or due to the unusually effective leadership of the manager or because the individual member of staff feels valued.

Most organisations are suffering from innovation overload. This is often happening just when staff morale is lowered because of redundancies and a general levelling of staff differentials. Staff respond to this in different ways. Some withhold commitment: see Scase and Goffee on how middle managers removed their commitment. Some withdraw from extra work. Some increase their militancy. Some simply bow their heads and resolve to work harder — again — like Boxer the horse in *Animal Farm*.

So what can organisations do about it? It is not usually possible to reduce the innovation overload. But, maybe, there is something that could be done about morale. There are several ways that people can help improve the morale of their team by valuing each other. Valuing is a complex social interaction which has something to do with valuing them as a person as well as the job which they do. Four types of valuing are consideration, feedback, delegation and consultation.

- *Consideration.* People tend to feel a lack of consideration from their colleagues when the organisational culture is one of keeping to oneself rather than talking to colleagues. Even at the simplest level such things as eye contact in corridors, good mornings, smiling and the everyday courtesies of the working day can make a difference. Evidence from research (Torrington and Weightman 1989) done in a variety of organisations suggests that most people would welcome more of these small gestures at work. Lack of consideration may be one of Herzberg's dissatisfiers.

- *Feedback.* We all appreciate some feedback about how well we are doing. This needs to be positive where possible but it also needs to include dealing with poor performance, otherwise the feedback has no credibility and can be just as demotivating as no feedback at all. Feedback is most appropriate as soon as possible after the performance and when it concentrates on the performance and not personal characteristics unless these affect the performance. See also Step 7.

- *Delegation.* Members of staff are valued when responsibility is delegated to them, but this involves delegating real responsibility, not just giving people jobs to do. Individuals must be trusted to make decisions about what, whether and how to do things, not just given tasks to complete. Otherwise they are likely to work to rule and feel like machines. Responsibility cannot be delegated and then taken away without devaluing confidence and future effectiveness. Mullins (1996, p. 570) suggests that delegation is founded on the concepts of:
  - authority — the right to make decisions and take actions
  - responsibility — the obligation to perform certain duties
  - accountability (ultimate responsibility) — cannot be delegated as the senior is ultimately responsible for the acts of the subordinates.

- *Consultation and participation.* Due to the innovation overload it is difficult to create the conditions in which people will respond to change with enthusiasm. However if they are to respond with commitment rather than stoical compliance then some sort of participation in at least the "how" even if not the "what" will help. Although it takes longer to get a decision if you involve more people, they are at least then committed to trying to make it work if they have been involved in the decision process. Whereas if you do not include people in the decision process it will take much longer to persuade them afterwards and they will often use all their creative powers to prove it cannot be done.

Valuing people through involvement and empowerment will increase their commitment and motivation to get things done. If they feel this is not really meant it will have the opposite effect, so any empowerment must be credible and not manipulative.

The use of design methodologies by what he calls "the human-centred enterprise" as a mean of dealing effectively with innovation overload is stressed by Andrew Jones in his book *The Innovation Acid Test.*

Summary Checklist

1. The power distribution in organisations will affect the relationships in them.
2. Empowering staff can increase commitment as long as it is not felt as being dumped on.
3. Empowerment and responsible autonomy require considerable investment in training and development.
4. Valuing staff can increase their motivation.

Step 6 Audit

	Rating						
	1	2	3	4	5	6	7
1. We empower our staff to take decisions about how they work.							
2. Our leaders are "joiners" not "tellers".							
3. We are considerate to one another in our actions.							
4. We give systematic feedback to each other formally and informally.							
5. Staff have real responsibility delegated to them.							
6. Staff are consulted about all decisions that affect them.							

Step 7

Do We Manage Performance so that People Know What Is Expected and Receive Feedback on their Own Performance?

If we are concerned with employee motivation we are by definition interested in employee performance, unless we are entirely employee-centred! Performance management became a management fad of the 1980s and 1990s with all sorts of schemes suggested. The reasons for the increased interest include:

- increased competitive pressures
- a clearer connection between organisational aims and individual targets
- restructuring of organisations with concomitant delegation of tasks
- a shift from collectivism to individualism.

The interest in performance management has continued and is still seen as a crucial management responsibility, even though there are growing doubts about adopting an overly mechanical approach to performance measurement.

Performance management can include the following attributes:

- communication about mission statements
- communication about business plans and progress
- Total Quality Management and other organisation-wide initiatives
- focus on senior management performance and connection with pay
- expected performance stated in terms of objectives or targets
- systematic performance appraisal
- performance related pay schemes
- formal ongoing reviews of progress identifying training needs.

Many organisations only use the last two or three of these and wonder why it becomes merely an administrative chore.

Torrington and Hall summarised the various aspects of performance management as a cycle of:

- determining performance expectations
- supporting performance both formally and informally
- reviewing and appraising performance
- managing performance standards.

Determining performance expectations includes all the various ways that organisations communicate what performance is expected. This includes formal methods such as job descriptions, procedures, business plans, briefing meetings and targets. It also includes informal methods such as the nudging and shaping of behaviour seen in many conversations and decisions at work. Employees seem to work best when their work is perceived as neither too difficult nor too easy. On the one hand they get stressed, on the other frustrated and bored. This perception about the challenge and their ability to cope is what counts, so consulting and involving employees is necessary to maximise motivation.

Supporting performance is the whole process of providing employees with the resources to do their job. It also includes the informal process of talking through aspects of the work and coaching people at work.

Reviewing and appraising performance has always been done informally. Formal reviews and appraisals are now commonplace with a wide range of methods available.

Managing performance standards includes dealing with any shortfalls that the review process has revealed. Training and development, absence management and changed resources are all included here.

There are associated problems with performance management, such as that focusing only on the appraisal process makes it merely historical. The process can become very bureaucratic and time-consuming. See *The Performance Management Audit* for more details on performance management.

Performance management assists in gaining employee commitment for two main reasons. First, people know what is expected of them and how this connects with what is going on elsewhere in the organisation. This allows people to see the meaning of what they are doing. Second, they receive feedback. All too often the enormous contribution and exhausting effort that people put into their jobs seems to lack any perceptible output. People need feedback from their colleagues. This can be the formal performance appraisal dealt with in performance management. It can also be informally taking an interest in what each other is doing. It is not hierarchy bound; a junior saying “That’s great! How do you do it?” can be very pleasing.

Summary Checklist

1. Performance management is more than performance appraisal.

2. Performance management includes expressing what is required, helping people to perform, reviewing the performance and dealing with the gap between expected and actual performance.

3. This process can assist in gaining commitment as individuals understand where they fit in and have the opportunity to evaluate their own effectiveness.

Step 7 Audit

	Rating						
	1	2	3	4	5	6	7
1. We communicate our performance expectations to staff through mission statements.							
2. We communicate our performance expectations to staff in business plans and the progress being made.							
3. We communicate our performance expectations through targets.							
4. We support our staff's performance through training and development.							
5. We support our staff's performance through ensuring suitable resources.							
6. Staff have their performance reviewed and appraised.							
7. We manage our performance standards consistently.							

Step 8

Does Our Organisation Improve, Adapt and Show Continuous Development?

Dealing with change has become an important part of organisational life and those that cope well are sometimes described as "learning organisations". These are organisations that continually improve and adapt to the new requirements of their circumstances. Organisations that manage to do this are attractive to employees in several ways. They are successful organisations, which are always more motivating to work in. Also, staying up to date with technology-related and other work skills increases the marketable competencies of individuals so they are at least employable even if they are not guaranteed lifelong employment from the same employer. Current skills are very useful on a CV.

The idea of a learning organisation was first articulated by Argyris and Schon and developed most notably by Peter Senge. It draws extensively on the approach advocated by "Systems Thinkers" like Russell Ackoff. Various lists, probably not quite well established enough yet to be called models, have been developed to describe these "learning organisations". Building an organisation's capacity to learn, according to Marquand and Reynolds, is based on the following:

- Transforming the individual and organisation's image of learning. The aim is to encourage lifelong learning and a desire for continuous improvement.
- Creating knowledge-based partnerships with people within and without the organisation to share ideas and information so a real understanding develops.
- Developing and expanding team learning activities to encourage people to share questions, information, ideas, solutions and approaches.
- Changing the role of managers to facilitators rather than controllers.
- Encouraging experiments and risk-taking so that new possibilities emerge rather than everyone playing things safe.
- Creating structures and systems with time to extract learning. This suggests some "soft" time for people to talk and develop rather than always being busy.
- Building opportunities and mechanisms to disseminate learning both formally and informally.
- Empowering people to take decisions and actions.

- Pushing information through the organisation and to external associates.
- Developing the discipline of system thinking, "what are the implications for others?".
- Creating a culture of continuous improvement.
- Developing a powerful vision of organisational excellence and individual fulfilment.
- Rooting out bureaucracy.

Pedlar, Burgoyne and Boydell suggest that the following features are indicative of a learning organisation, although they prefer the term "learning company" to "learning organisation":

- Learning approach to strategy — so that risks are taken and new opportunities are tried, so people learn about the new as well as the well-established.
- Participative policy-making with consultation and participation by people from all parts of the organisation.
- Open information systems — nothing is hidden from members of the organisation unless it is imperative.
- Formative, that is encouraging people, accounting and control rather than restrictive methods.
- Internal exchange of ideas and information.
- Flexibility of rewards so people can work to their own best way.
- Enabling structures for individual contributions.
- Boundary workers act as boundary scanners.
- Inter worker learning.
- Learning climate for all.
- Self-development opportunities for all.

These lists can seem a list of wishes rather than a practical guide to the reality of most organisations. Many would feel that not only are they unworkable but they could damage the viability of the organisation. However, the advantage of this learning organisation idea is that it can be a useful checklist for raising questions about an existing organisation. The ideas from the learning organisation approach have the advantage of opening up the discussion and using all the talents available to the organisation rather than relying on those at the top. In a competitive world those close to the customer are more likely to know what is really needed.

The concept of the learning organisation is helpful in encouraging us to look at the organisation as a whole and how the various functions and specialisms relate to each other. One way of looking at the learning organisation models is to see them as integrating models of managing people and ensuring that they are sufficiently motivated to give committed work and good performance.

Summary Checklist

1. A learning organisation tries to use the skills of all members and to develop these.
2. The learning organisation models draws in the holistic approach of Systems Thinking.
3. These learning organisation models can be seen as a way of integrating the people side of organisations.

Step 8 Audit

	Rating						
	1	2	3	4	5	6	7
1. We use a learning approach to strategy.							
2. We have participative policy-making.							
3. We have open information systems.							
4. We have formative accounting and control methods.							
5. We have an internal exchange of ideas and information.							
6. There is a flexibility of rewards.							
7. Our structures allow individual contributions.							
8. Our boundary workers act as boundary scanners.							
9. We have inter-worker learning.							
10. There is a learning climate.							
11. There are self-development opportunities.							

CONCLUSION

This audit has sought to suggest to you that there are various strands to gaining employee motivation and commitment. Having a clear idea of what is required and suitable rewards for doing so is at the heart of this process. People will differ in their personal interpretation of both the task and the rewards offered and the most effective organisations recognise these individual differences by talking and listening to people. The good leader is the one who knows the perceptions of the members of their team and melds these together to produce the excellent performance. When this fails absenteeism, sickness, poor work and low morale are the consequence.

Summary Checklist

The main areas in which organisations and managers can influence motivation at work are:

1. Acknowledge individual differences in how people learn and work and in what motivates them.

2. Cater for a range of needs including the primary security needs and the more complex secondary social and cultural needs.

3. Rewarding people for appropriate and desired behaviour will motivate those who wish to behave in these ways for these rewards.

4. Provide jobs that have variety, autonomy, interaction with others and responsibility.

5. Ensure that jobs enable people to practise and develop their competencies.

6. Allow for flexible working.

7. Make sure that managers are credible leaders.

8. Encourage effective teams with high levels of trust.

9. Empower staff and provide a balance of autonomous and heterarchical working.

10. Value staff.

11. Have performance management so that staff know what is expected of them and so that they can evaluate their own performance.

12. Have an organisation that allows people to learn and develop.

Part 3

The Audit Process

This section addresses the logistical and process requirements of conducting an audit. The topics covered in this section include:

- Staffing the audit team
- Creating an audit project plan
- Laying the groundwork for the audit
- Analysing audit results
- Sharing audit results
- Writing effective audit reports
- Dealing with resistance to audit recommendations
- Building an ongoing audit program.

STAFFING THE AUDIT TEAM

Who conducts the audit is as important in many ways as how the audit is conducted. In fact, the people selected for the audit team will, in large part, determine how the audit is done, how results are analysed, and how findings are reported. The following list includes general characteristics of effective audit teams for most areas:

- Consists of three to four people.
- Reports to CEO or other senior executive.
- Represents a carefully selected range of skills and experience.

More than four people may be needed for an audit team if data gathering is labor intensive, as when large numbers of customers or employees must be interviewed. However, audit teams of more than six or seven people present problems of maintaining uniformity and communicating audit progress and findings during the course of the evaluation.

Selecting an Audit Team Leader

The audit team leader will play a strong role in shaping both the data gathering and the findings from the audit. The strength of the team leader will also influence the acceptance of the audit, both in terms of enlisting cooperation in the data gathering phase and in securing support for improvement initiatives that grow out of the audit. Because of the importance of this role, care should be taken in selecting the appropriate person for the job. The following qualities are found in successful audit team leaders:

- Has a good relationship with the CEO or with the executive-level sponsor of the audit.
- Is well-liked and well-respected at all levels of the organisation, especially in the area to be audited.
- Has good interpersonal skills; can maintain good relationships even in difficult circumstances.

- Has good analytical skills; can assimilate and process large amounts of complex data quickly.
- Has some knowledge of the function or area being audited.
- Has extensive knowledge of the type of process being audited.
- Communicates ideas clearly and effectively.

Skills to be Represented on the Audit Team

Once the team leader has been chosen, audit team members should be selected on the basis of what each can bring to the project. Selection efforts should focus on developing a balanced representation of the following qualities:

- A variety of tenures in the organisation, with relative newcomers preferably having experience in other organisations.
- A variety of familiarity with the area (function or site) being audited. Those who are intimately familiar with the area can serve as guides to the less familiar; those who are new to the area can provide objectivity and ask questions that might never be considered by those more involved in the area.
- Considerable familiarity with the type of process being audited. For this reason, many organisations call on people filling roles in similar processes from other parts of the company to work on audit teams.
- Good analytical skills.
- Good interpersonal skills.
- Good facilitation and interviewing skills.
- Good communication skills.
- An understanding of the company's strategy and direction.

CREATING AN AUDIT PROJECT PLAN

Creating an audit project plan accomplishes the following objectives:

- Ensures the allocation of adequate resources, or helps audit team members be prepared to improvise in the face of short resources.
- Ensures the audit is timed so resources are available that may be in high demand.
- Creates clear expectations in the minds of team members about what must be done, and when — especially important when they are not committed to the project full-time.
- Ensures accountability for what must be done, who is responsible for which tasks, and when the audit must be completed.

Financial audits often rely on the Critical Path Method (CPM) of project planning. This method was originally developed by the US Department of Defense to facilitate the timely completion of weapons development and production. It has since been modified to plan a wide variety of projects. The following outline is a simplification of CPM. It suggests the aspects of a project that should be taken into account during the planning phase.

Critical Path Method

In developing the project plan, audit team members should ask and answer the following questions:

- *What tasks must be performed?*

This list should include the major tasks outlined in the audits, along with sub tasks that grow out of those major headings. It should also include any tasks mandated by unique circumstances in the company performing the self-assessment. The audit team may want to brainstorm about tasks that need to be performed, then refine the list to reflect the work priorities of the audit.

- *In what order will the tasks be completed?*

Answering this question should include an analysis of which tasks and sub tasks are dependent on others. Which tasks cannot begin until another has been completed? Which tasks can be done at any time? The audit team may want to place the ordered task on a time line, with start dates, expected duration of the step, and end dates outlined for each task.

- *Who will perform each task?*

Most tasks will be performed by members of the audit team. These assignments should be made by taking the strengths of each team member into consideration, as well as the time availability of each person. Equity of work load should also be taken into account. If tasks are to be assigned to people not on the audit team, those individuals should be included or consulted at this point.

- *What resources will be needed for each step?*

Each task should be analysed in terms of the personnel, budget, equipment, facilities, support services, and any other resources that will be needed for its completion. The team should assess the availability of all of the resources. Consideration should be given to the task ordering completed earlier. Are some resources subject to competing demands, and therefore difficult to secure at a particular time? How far in advance do arrangements for resources need to be made? Does the task order or time line need to be revised in light of what is known about resource availability?

- *Where is the slack time?*

Slack time is unscheduled time between dependent tasks. Slack provides a degree of flexibility in altering the start dates of subsequent tasks. Slack time signals that a task has a range of possible start dates. It is used to determine the critical path.

- *What is the critical path?*

The critical path in a project is the set of tasks that must be completed in a sequential, chronological order. If any task on the critical path is not completed, all subsequent tasks will be delayed. Delays at any point in the critical path will result in an equivalent delay in the completion of the total project.

Regardless of the method used to develop the project plan, no project, regardless how simple, is ever completed in exact accordance with its plan. However, having a project plan allows the team to gauge its progress, anticipate problems and determine where alternative approaches are needed.

LAYING THE GROUNDWORK FOR THE AUDIT

Once the team has been selected and a project plan developed, the audit leader should prepare those who will be involved in and affected by the audit for the team's visit or for data gathering. The following steps will help the audit to run more smoothly:

Communicate Executive Support for the Audit

Demonstrating executive support for the audit accomplishes two goals. First, it increases the chances that those involved in the area being audited will cooperate with data-gathering efforts. Second, it shows executive support for the area being audited and suggests a commitment to improving the area's performance.

In many companies, the audit is introduced by the executive sponsor of the audit by means of an intranet webcast or a more conventional written or multimedia presentation. The presentation should explain the purpose of the audit and ask for the support of everyone in the area being audited. It should be seen by everyone within the company who will be affected by or involved in the data gathering process. The most effective presentations explain how the audit results will be used, reassuring those who will be responding to audit team requests about the motives of the audit. Credibility is also bolstered when previous audits have been acted upon with positive results.

Make Arrangements with the Area to Be Audited

The audit team leader should check with the appropriate manager in charge of the process or site being audited to arrange for any required on-site visits, interviewing, surveys, focus groups, or written information needed for the audit. The team leader should also explain the purpose, scope, and expected duration of the audit; review the project plan with the manager; and answer any questions the manager has about the audit.

The team leader should also work with the appropriate manager or managers to determine how the audit can be conducted with the least impact on the flow of work. This may include discussions about the timing of the audit, the options for data gathering, the availability of needed data, and possibilities for generating the necessary information quickly and easily. Finding ways to make data collection more efficient and effective is especially important when the audit is part of an ongoing program, rather than an isolated assessment.

Develop a Protocol or Checklist

A protocol or checklist can be used by the audit team to outline the issues that are central to the audit. Written guides can help the leaders of those areas being audited to prepare for the audit. A protocol represents a plan of what the audit team will do to accomplish the objectives of the audit. It is an important tool of the audit, since it not only serves as the audit team's guide to collecting data, but also as a record of the audit procedures completed by the team. In many cases, audit teams may want to format the checklist in a way that allows them to enter their field notes directly on an electronic checklist.

The checklist should include no more than twenty major items, and checklists should be updated with each audit in order to ensure that the appropriate measures are taken. Items where improvement initiatives have been successful should be eliminated from the checklist, with newly identified possibilities for improvement opportunities added.

ANALYSING AUDIT RESULTS

Discovering gaps between a company's targets and its actual performance is a relatively easy task. Tools are provided to assist audit teams in assessing their performance in a given area. In most cases, more opportunities for improvement will be uncovered by an audit than can be addressed by the resources and energy available. Therefore, one of the most difficult aspects of analysing the results of an audit lies in determining which opportunities are the most important for managers to pursue.

Because resources and energy for pursuing improvement initiatives are limited, choices must be made about which options are most important. Sometimes these decisions are based on political winds in the company, or on what has worked well in the past, or on personal preferences of top management. However, scarce resources will be used more effectively if allocated to the areas where they will have the greatest impact. Managers must also determine the most effective way to approach initiatives. This section discusses criteria for prioritising opportunities that grow out of audit findings.

The Novations Strategic Alignment Model

For many years, the "excellence" movement, encouraged companies to achieve excellence in every area of endeavor. Although the movement created an awareness of the need for management improvements, it failed to consider that not all management processes are equal in terms of producing benefits. As a result, leading organisations in today's environment focus on performing well in a few core areas. Knowing what those core areas are depends on a clear vision of the company's strategy.

Strategic thinking about which areas should be improved involves much more than taking an inventory of current capabilities and weaknesses. If it did not, existing capabilities would always determine strategic objectives, and organisational growth and development would come to a halt. To set priorities strategically, companies must decide which improvement opportunities fall in the following categories:

- What to do themselves.
- What to do with someone else.
- What to contract others to do.
- What not to do.

FIGURE 1
CATEGORIES OF WORK

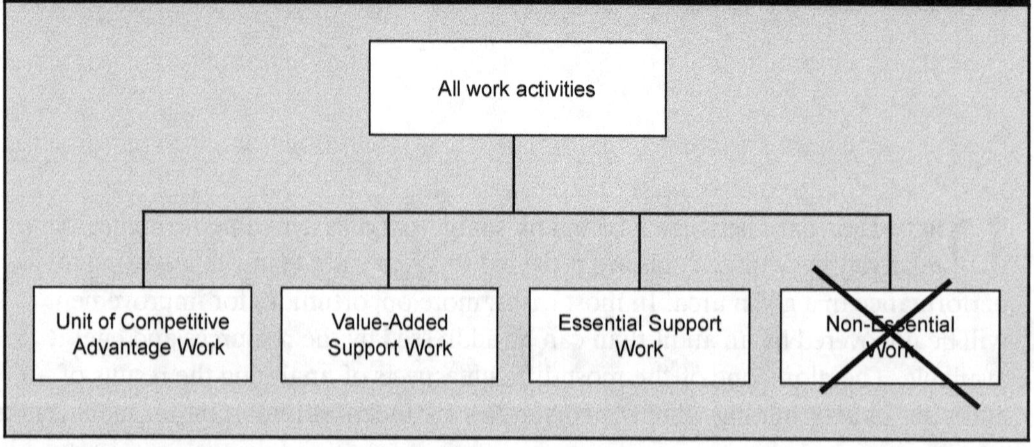

Figure 1 illustrates the four categories of work.

Unit of Competitive Advantage (UCA) Work includes work and capabilities that create distinctiveness for the business in the marketplace.

Value-added Support Work facilitates the accomplishment of the UCA work. For example, a company may have a technology orientation rather than a service orientation, but an effective logistics process may help them to improve their UCA work of providing cutting-edge technology.

Essential Support Work neither creates advantage nor facilitates the work that creates advantage, but must be done if businesses are to continue to operate (includes such things as paying taxes, maintaining payroll records, etc.).

Nonessential Work is activity that has lost its usefulness but continues to be done because of tradition.

Despite their sophistication in dealing with other aspects of business, most managers have archaic views of the different types of work. Many of their models for characterising work have come from a finance or accounting orientation. Accounting terms such as overhead, direct labor, and indirect labor may be useful as a way to report costs, but they provide little understanding about the relative strategic importance of the work. Yet these classifications are frequently used to determine how work is organised and where resources are allocated.

The concept of *unit of competitive advantage* (UCA) helps to explain why some organisations either emphasise the wrong capabilities or de-emphasise the right capabilities. UCA also explains why some forms of improvement lead to competitive disadvantage, and why some businesses consistently outperform their competitors by gaining greater leverage from their competitive advantages.

A company's UCA includes the critical processes that create distinctiveness within an established strategic direction. It is based on the premise that businesses create competitive advantage when they focus their attention on a few key processes and implement those key processes in world-class fashion. For example, continuous improvement is a popular management program that assumes benefit from any kind of ongoing improvement. Generally speaking, however, continuous improvement programs will only create competitive advantage when an organisation defines a strategic direction, clarifies strategic objectives, and determines its UCA. These crucial prerequisites tell where continuous improvement efforts should be focused to create maximum leverage. They suggest what kinds of work to improve interdependently, what kinds to improve separately, and what kinds not to waste time on. They even signal when continuous improvement is more likely to create competitive disadvantage rather than competitive advantage.

UCA Initiatives Should Take Priority

Understanding what work falls under which categories requires a clear understanding of the company's strategy. The initiatives resulting from an audit that affect the Unit of Competitive Advantage work processes should clearly have the highest priority among improvement projects. Value-added support initiatives should be second priority, and essential support work should be the third priority. Nonessential work should not be continued.

Once improvement opportunities that will have the greatest impact on the achievement of the company's goals have been identified, the following ideas can be used to lend further insight into how opportunities identified through an audit should be prioritised:

- *Focus on the two or three most important areas.*

Insisting that action be taken on all of the problems uncovered by the audit may overwhelm the people who are responsible for bringing about those changes. Flatter organisations and leaner work forces mean that people are already being asked to do more work with fewer resources and less time. Producing a long list of improvement initiatives may prompt people to dismiss all of them because they don't have time to complete the whole list.

- *Focus on the areas that can be changed.*

Emphasising problems that are beyond the control of the people who are responsible to work on process improvement only leads to cynicism and a sense of powerlessness. By focusing on things that are within the sphere of influence, accountability for each part of the action plan can be clearly defined.

- *Include as priorities some improvements that can be made quickly.*

Rapid, visible improvement helps build support for more complicated initiatives. Quick improvements also reassure people of management's support for long-term improvement. Seeing immediate improvement helps to build commitment at all levels to the process, and helps build momentum for further change.

- *Emphasise the improvements that seem essential to long-term success.*

Essential improvements may involve sensitive issues or difficult problems, such as deficiencies in fundamental skill levels within the organisation or basic strategy issues. These problems are not only difficult and expensive to address, but may also cause a great deal of personal pain or require significant individual adjustment. Nevertheless, long-term improvement requires a commitment to dealing with difficult issues rather than avoiding them.

SHARING AUDIT RESULTS

In most cases, audit results will be presented to various interested people in a feedback meeting before they are made available online. Those in attendance may include members of the executive team, managers who work in the area covered by the audit, the audit team members, and anyone else who is affected by or interested in the results. The meeting should be conducted by members of the audit team. The purpose is to present their findings, and make recommendations for capitalising on opportunities for improvement.

Conducting Effective Feedback Meetings

The audit team's strategy for the meeting should be to present a clear and simple picture of the current situation as revealed by the audit. This may be a moment of truth for those who have been anticipating the audit results. The feedback meeting for an audit holds both excitement and anxiety: excitement that the future will be bright, and anxiety that shortcomings in individual performance will be highlighted and demands made for personal change. As a result, the meeting must be carefully managed in order to lead to productive change. The following structure is one recommended format for conducting a feedback meeting.

- *Introduce the meeting and preview its agenda.*

This might include an overview of the original intent of the audit, introduction of the audit team, and a brief summary of the meeting's agenda. This step should take no more than five minutes.

- *Present the audit findings.*

Audit findings should summarise the most important points revealed by the data gathered in the audit process. They should be presented separately from the audit recommendations in order to allow people to digest the two parts of the presentation separately. Clearing up misunderstandings about the findings may make the group more accepting of the team's recommendations.

The presentation of the audit findings should take comparatively little time. Audits almost always generate much more data than can be effectively presented or digested in a feedback meeting. The goal of the audit team should be to zero in on the two or three most important points learned from the audit, and present enough supporting data to illustrate those points.

Presenting too much data about audit findings has a number of negative effects. It encourages people to conduct their own analysis of the audit data. To a certain extent, this is a healthy and normal reaction. If others understand the evidence that supports the conclusions drawn by the audit team, they are more likely to accept and own the audit results. Therefore, they will be more committed to the changes brought about by the audit results. However, when people immerse themselves in large amounts of data, they may become victims of "analysis paralysis": they may spend unnecessary time attempting to explain contradictory data, or trying to understand methods used by others to gather data.

- *Present audit recommendations.*

Presenting the audit recommendations should be the central point of the meeting. The recommendations should grow out of the data highlights presented. The audit team should view the recommendations as discussion points for the meeting, rather than as absolute action items.

A common mistake in feedback meetings is to spend most of the meeting on presenting data and recommendations. It is easy for audit team members to become enamored of data they have invested considerable time and energy to collect and analyse. Others in the audience will probably also be interested in the details of the data collected. However, if too much time is spent on discussing the recommendations, the meeting will end before a commitment to action has been made.

- *Ask others to react to the data.*

The reactions of top management and those responsible for implementing audit recommendations will determine the ultimate value of the audit data. Therefore, the feedback meeting is a good time to resolve questions or problems with the findings and recommendations as they have been presented. If resistance to the audit findings is not resolved in the feedback meeting, opportunities for improvement may be lost.

Those attending the meeting may offer their opinions willingly. If not, the audit team members should ask the others in the room for their reaction to what has been presented.

- *Develop preliminary action plans.*

The detailed action plans should grow out of the recommendations made by the audit team. They should specifically address the question of who should do what by when. Formal accountability mechanisms should be established before the end of the meeting, such as the scheduling of subsequent meetings or follow-up check points.

Sharing reports more widely

The same rules that apply to the critical feedback meeting apply to the sharing of audit results across the organisation.

While it is important to make the key data, principle conclusions and preliminary action plans quickly and available online, it is distracting and unhelpful to provide or circulate too much data. Once again, staff are likely to be distracted by the possibility of over-analysing the data or engaging in protracted discussion of alternative interpretations when they don't fully understand the nature if the process being audited.

Of course, it is also important that the staff involved in the departments and processes that have been audited should not feel blamed for systematic problems or weaknesses. On the contrary, the most effective presentation of audit results will clearly highlight improvements that can result from the audit and generate enthusiasm for the audit process in other areas of the organisation. The next section contains further information on this topic.

PREPARING EFFECTIVE AUDIT REPORTS

There are three fundamental purposes for preparing a formal report at the conclusion of an audit:

- An audit report may be a stand-alone summary of the audit. This approach is not recommended, inasmuch as the report is likely to be filed away, making the probability of action unlikely.
- The report may supplement a feedback meeting, providing those in attendance with documentation and an outline to follow.
- The report should also serve as a baseline document to make measurement of performance improvement possible in future audits.

Because the written report is the most enduring part of the audit presentation, it should be well written and easy to understand. The following tips will lead to the preparation of effective written audit reports.

Focus on a Few Key Points

The audit presentation should focus on the two or three most important findings. It is impossible to present all of the data gathered in the audit to those who were not on the audit team. It is also not advisable to present every detail of the data. The audit team members should trust their own judgment about what the highlights of the study were, and present enough data to support that judgment. For each of the major findings, the team may want to include the following information:

- What is the problem?
- Why does it exist?
- What happens if the problem is not fixed:
  - in the short term?
  - in the long term?
- Recommend solutions.
- Outline expected benefits.

Prepare an Outline Before Preparing the First Draft

A good outline ensures that the logic of the report is clear, and that ideas proceed in an order that makes sense. The following outline provides one approach that works effectively.

Background

This section should establish the framework for the audit in terms of:

- Providing a brief discussion of the overall purpose of the audit.
- Identifying the role of the audit team in the overall process.
- Establishing the limitations of the audit methodology to ensure that others utilise the results provided in the report appropriately.

Objectives

This section should identify specific objectives of the audit in terms of types of information the team was expected to generate.

Methodology

The methodology section should describe the mechanics of the audit and include the following information:

- Types of assessment used (survey, interviews, focus groups, etc.).
- Data sources, or the sample groups for each of the types of assessment used.
- Time frame during which the audit was conducted.
- Other pertinent details about how the audit was conducted.

Findings

This section is designed to provide others with a review of the "facts" that came out of the audit. Except in cases where an audit checks regulatory compliance, only the most significant findings should be discussed in any detail in the report. This section should also include briefly presented data supporting the findings.

Conclusions

This section should report the audit team's interpretation of what the facts of the audit mean in light of the objectives stated at the outset of the audit.

Recommendations

This section includes suggestions from the audit team on how to close the performance gaps identified in the audit. The degree of specificity to be included in the audit report will vary from company to company and audit to audit.

Appendix

This portion of the formal report should include any of the following items that are relevant to the audit:

- A copy of any questionnaires or survey instruments used in the audit.
- A summary of the data gathered in the course of the audit.
- Recommendations for subsequent audits based on the team's experience.

Present Audit Findings Accurately

Those who read the report will no doubt be somewhat familiar with the area covered by the audit. They may notice discrepancies between what they know about the subject and what is reported in the written document. Spotting one inaccuracy may lead the readers to discredit all of the findings, conclusions and recommendations. Audit team members should be careful to report data as it was actually generated, and to describe the impact of the findings accurately.

Use Clear, Concise Language

Every statement included in the report should be based on sound evidence developed or reviewed during the audit. Whatever is said must be supported or supportable. Speculation should be avoided. Generalities and vague reporting will only confuse and mislead those that the report should influence or inform. For example, a report using the terms *some*, *a few*, or *not all* can leave the reader confused about the significance of the finding. Specific quantities should be used, such as, "of the ten samples taken, two were found to be...", "Three of five respondents said that...", and so on. Statements should be qualified as needed, and any unconfirmed data or information should be identified as such.

Ideas that do not amplify the central theme should be eliminated. The report should not identify individuals or highlight the mistakes of individuals.

Use Good Grammar and Style

Basic rules should be followed in preparing the report. Below are some examples:

- Avoid extreme terms, such as alarming, deplorable, gross negligence, etc.
- Avoid using redundant or lengthy phrases, such as calling something an emergency situation when the word emergency alone will do.
- Avoid verbs camouflaged as nouns or adjectives. For example, use "the new procedure will reduce error entries," rather than "The new procedure will accomplish a reduction of error entries."
- Avoid indirect expressions where possible. For example, "Many instances of poor management were found" is more direct than saying, "There were many instances of poor judgment found".
- Use short, familiar words. Use words that are easily understandable to everyone and that convey the message concisely.
- Keep sentences short. Most writing experts suggest that an average sentence should be between 15 and 18 words. Packing too many ideas into a single sentence confuses and tires readers.

The audit team should provide enough background information in the report so that the reader clearly understands who conducted the audit and what the audit did or did not include. The purpose of the report as well as the purpose and scope of the audit should also be described in a manner that enables the reader to know why the report was written and who should take corrective action.

Timing of the Report

The timing of audit reports is critical to the overall reporting process and must be carefully thought out. In many cases, a written draft of the audit report is prepared one to three weeks before the feedback meeting. This draft then goes through a review and another report is prepared in time for the team's presentation. A final report may be completed after the feedback session has been held in order to record changes resulting from that meeting.

Presentation of the Report

The audit report will probably be made available on the company intranet to all interested employees, often with a short summary linking to more detailed conclusions and relevant audit data.

However, just as the audit program will normally have been introduced by means of a webcast or similar online presentation, so it will be useful for the same individual to make a brief presentation of the audit's conclusions. This will provide a measure of continuity and ensure that the audit team has the chance to emphasise the benefits of the audit to the business as a whole and to reassure those staff who may have lingering concerns that the audit is a veiled attempt to justify cut-backs or job-losses. A live question and answer session will also be useful if team members sense significant levels of concern or resistance amongst staff (see the next section)

Presented thoughtfully, the audit results can help to underline the company's commitment to its strategic objectives and help to generate increased commitment and participation at all levels of the organisation.

DEALING WITH RESISTANCE TO RECOMMENDATIONS

Most audit teams feel that if they can present their ideas clearly and logically, and have the best interests of the company or department at heart, managers will accept the recommendations made as part of the audit and follow the team's recommendations. Many people who have worked in organisations, however, find that no matter how reasonably recommendations are presented, they are all too often not implemented.

Implementation usually fails because it requires people to change their ways of working. That change requires a great deal of effort, energy, and risk; therefore, change is usually resisted. Resistance is an emotional process; people may embrace recommendations based on their logic, but fail to implement them because of the emotional resistance to the personal change involved. Resistance is a predictable, natural, and necessary part of the learning process. Although resistance may cause audit team members to feel they have missed the mark in terms of the recommendations they have made, it actually often signals accuracy in having interpreted the organisation's needs. By dealing with the resistance directly, audit teams can work through barriers to implementing process improvements.

What Are the Signs of Resistance?

In many cases, resistance may be expressed directly. Direct objections to recommendations are relatively easy to address, inasmuch as they can be discussed and resolved. When recommendations are being presented in the initial meeting, team members should stop frequently to allow those who are listening to the report to voice any objections or disagreements. Those who are presenting the data should be careful not to become defensive or to punish those who express reservations about the recommendations. It is impossible to deal with objections unless they are voiced; therefore, the audit team should welcome the expression of objections or differences of opinion. The following tips may be used for surfacing and dealing with direct resistance:

- Provide many opportunities for others to express their concerns.
- Carefully clarify any confusing concerns.
- Deal with important or easy concerns immediately. Defer the remainder.
- Summarise the concerns before moving on. Show that concerns have been heard.

If direct resistance continues, the following steps may be necessary:

- Talk about the differences of opinion.
- Voice concern and support for negotiating a resolution.
- Avoid struggles for control of the situation.

Dealing with Indirect Resistance

In other cases, resistance may be subtle and elusive. Indirect resistance is difficult to identify and deal with because its manifestations seem logical. People who are experiencing indirect resistance may feel that they are "getting the run around". Many different forms of resistance may manifest themselves at the first meeting or more widely across the company:

- Request for more detail.
- Providing too much detail in response to questions.
- Complaining that there isn't enough time to implement recommendations.
- Claiming that the recommendations are impractical.
- Attacking those who propose improvement initiatives.
- Acting confused.
- Responding with silence.
- Intellectualising about the data.
- Moralising that problems wouldn't exist if it weren't for "those people".
- Agreeing to implement recommendations with no intention of acting on them.
- Asking questions about methodology.
- Arguing that previous problems have resolved themselves.
- Focusing on solutions before findings are fully understood.

Almost any of these responses is legitimate in moderate amounts. For example, members of the group may have concerns about the audit's methodology that should be considered. Managers may realistically wonder where they will find the time to implement recommendations. However, if refusal to act on recommendations persists once legitimate concerns have been addressed, then the audit team is probably facing indirect resistance.

Many models used in sales training provide recommendations for overcoming resistance. These methods suggest the use of data and logical arguments to win the point and convince the other person to buy whatever is being sold. These models work well for direct resistance. However, indirect resistance is normally based on feelings rather than logic. Therefore, the only way to truly overcome resistance is to deal with the emotional processes that cause it to happen in the first place. It is almost impossible to talk people out of the way they feel.

Feelings pass and change when they are expressed directly. A key skill for audit teams that are attempting to implement recommendations is to ask the people who are presenting resistance to put directly into words what they are experiencing. The most effective way to make this happen is for the audit team members to address directly what is happening in the situation. The following keys provide help in surfacing and dealing with indirect resistance.

- *Work once or twice with the person's concern, even when it feels as if be or she is resisting recommendations.*

By attempting to work with the problem stated by the person raising a concern, audit team members can determine whether the concern is legitimate or whether it is an excuse for not taking action. If the issues raised are legitimate, the person should show some willingness to discuss and resolve them. If the issues are manifestations of indirect resistance, the person will probably respond with other forms of resistance.

- *Identify the form the resistance is taking.*

Paying attention to the dynamics of a discussion can provide important clues as to whether or not a person is resisting recommendations. If a person is consistently distancing him or herself from those who are presenting the audit findings, using gestures or postures that suggest tension or discomfort, while at the same time presenting arguments for why the recommendations presented are inappropriate, it is probably a sign of resistance. The non-verbal responses of the presenters may also signal the onset of resistance. If presenters feel that they are suppressing negative feelings or becoming bored or irritated, it may be further evidence that the client is resisting.

Once presenters become aware of the resistance, the next step is to put it into words. This is best done by using neutral, everyday language. The skill is to describe the form of the resistance in a way that encourages the person to make a more direct statement of the reservation he or she is experiencing.

One general rule for stating what type of resistance is being manifested is to phrase the statement in common, non-threatening language. Statements should be made in the same tone and language that would be used to address a problem with a spouse or close friend. The statement should be made with as little evaluation as possible; it is the presenter's observation about what is happening in the situation.

A second general rule for surfacing indirect resistance involves not talking for a couple of moments after the presenter has stated what he or she has observed. There may be a temptation to elaborate on the observation, or to support it with evidence. However, continuing the statement will reduce the tension in the situation. Without tension, the person who is resisting feels no discomfort, and is unlikely to address the issue directly. Moreover, elaborating on the original statement may increase the other person's defensiveness and reduce the chances of solving the problem.

If stating the problem in direct, non-punishing terms fails to bring the resistance out into the open, there may be little more the audit team can do to overcome the indirect resistance. The best strategy in this case is to avoid resisting the resistance. Team members should support the person who is resisting and proceed with the implementation of recommendations to the extent possible.

BUILDING AN ONGOING AUDIT PROGRAM

As the pace of change increases, and as organisation leaders become more and more committed to continuously improving their effectiveness and efficiency, audits of all types of processes will become more common. The most effective companies will establish programs of ongoing audits, whereby a number of goals can be accomplished:

- Performance improvements can be measured over time.
- Important changes in the company's environment can be systematically monitored.
- Managers can make a habit of change and improvement, rather than resisting it.
- Those areas that are of highest importance to the company can be routinely improved.
- Processes can be modified to be in alignment with changes in strategy or in the environment.

As with all management techniques, however, an enduring program of ongoing audits requires that audits become integrated into the overall management system. The following guidelines are keys to weaving audits into the fabric of day-to-day operations.

Establish Support for Ongoing Audits

While support for audits begins at the executive level, ownership for the audit process must be felt throughout the organisation if an ongoing program is to be successful. The following actions will help to broaden support for the audit process, while ensuring greater benefit from the audit.

- *Share the results of the audit with everyone throughout the organisation.*

By keeping others informed about the results of an audit, managers reassure those who participate in and are affected by the audit of the integrity of the process. Employees sometimes become suspicious of probing investigators; they may have doubts about how the information will be used, or whether the information will be used. By sharing audit results, managers make an implicit commitment to improving the processes that have been evaluated.

- *Act on the audit results.*

Questions will be raised about continuing audits if early assessments bear no fruits. Failing to act on performance gaps that are identified leads to cynicism and lack of trust among those who work with the problems daily. On the other hand, improving a process can create the momentum that comes from accomplishment. Committing resources and attention to the improvement opportunities revealed by an audit also shows management commitment to the improvement process.

- *Let others know when performance has improved.*

Communicating the positive results from an audit is one way of rewarding the people who contributed to that improvement. It also builds faith in the effectiveness of the audit process. Moreover, showing that performance has improved is another means of reassuring people of a commitment to the improvement process.

- *Reward people for their part in improvements.*

Increasing efficiency and effectiveness can often be a threatening experience for those who are involved in a work process. Improving the way resources are used often means eliminating the need for some of the people who have been involved in the process. Although flatter, leaner organisations often preclude the possibility of offering promotions, managers should nevertheless attempt to ensure that people who contribute to performance improvement find their own situations better rather than worse as a result.

Rewards for helping to close performance gaps may span a range from thanking people for their efforts to planning a group celebration to offering bonuses or pay increases for improvement. Rewards are especially meaningful when people are allowed to suggest what rewards they would like for their contribution. This may provide managers with new ideas for rewards that may be less costly to the organisation than financial recognition.

- *Involve a wide variety of people in the audit process.*

People can be involved in the audit process in many ways. By involving people from a broad spectrum, more people learn about audit techniques and results, thus spreading commitment to the audit process throughout the organisation. By involving many people in the data-gathering process, employees feel that action plans growing out of the audit were a result of their input. Excluding people from the data-gathering phase usually reduces the feeling of ownership for the results, thus making people feel as if initiatives are being imposed on them. By the same token, involving a broad range of people in the development of action plans expands ownership for the plans and allows for the generation of more ideas.

REFERENCES

Ackoff, R. L., Addison, H. J. and Bibb, S., *Management F-Laws: How organizations really work*, Triarchy Press, 2007.

Adair, J., *Action Centred Leadership*, Gower, 1982.

Adams, J. S., "Injustice in Social Exchange", in R. M. Steers and L. W. Porter (eds) *Motivation and Work Behaviour*, 2nd Edition, McGraw Hill, 1979.

Argyris, C, and Schon, D., *Organizational Learning*, Addison-Wesley, 1978.

Armstrong, M., *Employee Reward*, Institute of Personnel and Development, 1996.

Armstrong, M. *The Performance Management Audit*, *Cambridge Strategy Publications*, 2003.

Barham, K., *The Teams Audit*, Cambridge Strategy Publications, 2002.

Belbin, R. M., *Management Teams*: why they succeed or fail, Heinemann, 1981.

Bibb, S., and Kourdi, J., *A Question of Trust*, Cyan, 2007.

Bibb, S., James, J. and Walker, S., *Generation Y: What they want from work*, Triarchy Press, 2008.

Blake, R. R. and Mouton, J. S., *Building a Dynamic Organization through Grid Organization Development*, Gull, 1969.

Bristow, N., Buckner, K., Folkman, J. and McKinnon, P., *The Leadership Skills Audit*, Cambridge Strategy Publications, 2003.

Buchanan, D. and Huczynski, J., *Organisational Behaviour,* 3rd Edition, Prentice Hall, 1997.

Burns, J. M., *Leadership*, Harper and Row, 1978.

Carey, A., *Project Red Stripe*, Triarchy Press, 2008.

Equal Opportunities Commission, *Equal pay for work of equal value: a guide to the amended Equal Fay Act*, EOC, 1995.

Etzioni, A., *A Comparative Analysis of Complex Organizations: On power, involvement and their correlates*, Revised Edition, Free Press, 1975.

Fairtlough, G., *No Secrets!: Innovation through openness*, Triarchy Press, 2008.

Fairtlough, G., *The Three Ways of Getting Things Done*, International Edition, Triarchy Press, 2007.

Fiedler, F. E., *A Theory of Leadership Effectiveness*, McGraw Hill, 1967.

Goldthorpe, J. H., Lockwood, D., Bechhofer, F. and Platt, J., *The Affluent Worker in the Class Struggle*, Cambridge University Press, 1969.

Guirdham, M., *Interpersonal Skills at Work*, Prentice Hall, 1990.

Hackman, J. R., "Work Design", in R. M. Steers and L. W Porter (eds) *Motivation and Work Behaviour*, 4th Edition, McGraw Hill, 1987.

Herzberg, E, "One More Time: How do you motivate employees?" *Harvard Business Review*, January/February 1968.

Houston, R., *The Organisational Change Audit*, Cambridge Strategy Publications, 2003.

Hyman, J. and Cunningham, I., "Empowerment in Organisations: changes in the manager's role", in D. Megginson and S. Gibb (eds) *Managers as Developers*, Prentice Hall, 1996.

Janis, I. L., *Victims of Groupthink*, Houghton Mifflin, 1972.

Jones, A., *The Innovation Acid Test*, Triarchy Press, 2008.

Kotter, J., *The General Managers*, Free Press, 1982.

Krech, D., Crutchfield, R. S. and Ballachey, E. L., *Individual in Society*, McGraw Hill, 1962.

Kuhnert, K. W and Lewis, P., "Transactional and Transformational Leadership: a constructive/developmental analysis", *Academy of Management Review*, October 1987, pp. 648-57.

Lawler, E., "The Strategic Design of Reward Systems", in C. Fombrun, N. Tichy and A. Devanna (eds) *Strategic Human Resource Management*, Wiley, 1984.

Leigh, T. and Brown, S., *Journal of Applied Psychology*, August 1996.

Lewin, K., *Field Theory in Social Science*, Tavistock Publications, 1952.

Locke, E. A., "Towards a Theory of Task Motivation and Incentives", *Organizational Behaviour and Human Performance*, Vol. 3, 1968.

Marchington, M. and Wilkinson, A., *Core Personnel and Development*, Institute of Personnel and Development, 1996.

Marquand, M. and Reynolds, A., *The Global Learning Organisation*, Irwin, 1994.

Maslow, A. H., *Motivation and Personality*, Harper and Row, 1954.

Mills, C. W, *White Collar: the American middle classes*, Oxford University Press, 1956.

Mintzberg, H., *The Nature of Managerial Work*, Harper and Row, 1973.

Mullins, L. J., *Management and Organisational Behaviour*, Pitman, 1996.

Pedlar, M., Burgoyne, J. and Boydell, T, *The Learning Company: A strategy for sustained development*, McGraw Hill, 1991.

Pfeffer, J., *Power in Organizations*, Pitman, 1981.

Scase, R. and Goffee, R., *Reluctant Managers*, Unwin Hyman, 1989.

Senge, P., *The Fifth Discipline*, Nicholas Brealey Publishing Ltd., 1994.

Steers, R. M. and Porter, L. W (eds), *Motivation and Work Behaviour*, 4th Edition, McGraw Hill, 1987.

Steers, R. M. and Porter, L. W (eds), *Motivation and Work Behaviour*, 5th Edition, McGraw Hill, 1991.

Stewart, R., *Managers and their Jobs*, Macmillan, 1967.

Tannenbaum, R. and Schmidt, W H., "How to Choose a Leadership Pattern", *Harvard Business Review*, May-June 1973, pp. 162-75, 178-180.

Tate, W., *The Organisational Leadership Audit*, Cambridge Strategy Publications, 2003.

Torrington, D. and Hall, L., *Personnel Management: Human Resource Management in Action*, Prentice Hall, 1995.

Torrington, D. and Weightman, J., "Technical Atrophy in Middle Management", *Journal of General Management*, vol. 7(4), 1982, pp. 5-17.

Torrington, D. and Weightman, J., "The Analysis of Management Work" *Training and Management Development Methods*, vol. 1, 1987, pp. 27-33.

Torrington, D. and Weightman, J., *The Reality of School Management*, Blackwell, 1989.

Tuckman, B. W, "Development Sequences in Small Groups", *Psychological Bulletin*, 63, 1965, pp. 384-99.

Turner, A. and Lawrence, P., *Industrial Jobs and the Worker*, Harvard University Graduate School of Business Administration, 1965.

Vroom V. and Deci, E., *Management and Motivation*, Penguin, 1974.

Vulpian, A., *Towards The Third Modernity*, Triarchy Press, 2008.

Weightman, J., *Middle Management: Dinosaur or Dynamo?* PhD thesis, UMIST, 1986.

ABOUT THE AUTHOR

Jane Weightman is an independent author, researcher and trainer in human resources management. Formerly a researcher and honorary lecturer at UMIST's School of Management in Manchester, she has conducted numerous studies and provided considerable advice on the development of management competencies in both the public and private sector in the UK and internationally. Jane is the author of over 12 books on a variety of HR topics (five of them co-authored with Professor Derek Torrington of UMIST) and a regular contributor to journals.

ABOUT THE PUBLISHER

Business and Management Resources for forward-thinking organisations

Whatever name you give it, your organisation is almost certainly looking for new ways to *outsmart competitors *win and keep customers *develop new products or services *train and motivate staff *cut costs and delays *increase profits.

Cambridge Strategy Publications has a highly-respected — and rapidly-growing — range of management resources to help you do exactly that. Now being used in more than 90 countries around the world, by organisations large and small and in every business sector, CSP's management resources will help you implement change fast in your organisation.

- If you want to measure performance and implement appropriate change in any area of your business — look at our range of self-assessment audits. They cover all aspects of Marketing, Human Resources and Strategic Business Management. Visit www.cambridgestrategy.com or contact us at the address below.
- If you want to harness the power of High-Performance Teams, Total Quality, Benchmarking or Project-Based Reengineering — turn to our Portfolios in these areas. Each contains project guides and planners and a range of tools that you can put to work right away.
  Visit www.cambridgestrategy.com or contact us at the address below.
- If you want to share your experience of conducting this audit or get in touch with other organisations who have also used it — try our online audit network.
  Visit www.cambridgestrategy.com/networking or contact us at the address below.

Cambridge Strategy Publications Ltd.
Station Offices
Station Yard
Axminster
Devon. EX13 5PF.
United Kingdom

Tel: +44 (0)1297 631456
Fax: +44 (0)1297 631456
info@cambridgestrategy.com
www.cambridgestrategy.com